# Eva PenzeyMoog

# DESIGN FOR SAFETY

## MORE FROM A BOOK APART

**Voice Content and Usability**
*Preston So*

**Better Onboarding**
*Krystal Higgins*

**Sustainable Web Design**
*Tom Greenwood*

**Design for Cognitive Bias**
*David Dylan Thomas*

**Cross-Cultural Design**
*Senongo Akpem*

**Expressive Design Systems**
*Yesenia Perez-Cruz*

**Resilient Management**
*Lara Hogan*

**Everyday Information Architecture**
*Lisa Maria Marquis*

**Progressive Web Apps**
*Jason Grigsby*

**Flexible Typesetting**
*Tim Brown*

Visit abookapart.com for our full list of titles.

Publisher: Jeffrey Zeldman
Designer: Jason Santa Maria
Executive director: Katel LeDû
Managing editor: Lisa Maria Marquis
Editors: Sally Kerrigan, Adaobi Obi Tulton
Book producer: Ron Bilodeau

ISBN: 978-1-952616-09-9

A Book Apart
New York, New York
http://abookapart.com

10 9 8 7 6 5 4 3 2 1

# TABLE OF CONTENTS

1   *Introduction*

4   CHAPTER 1
Overcoming Our Assumptions

14   CHAPTER 2
Who's in Control?

33   CHAPTER 3
The Dangers of Location-Revealing Data

52   CHAPTER 4
Surveillance and the Struggle for Privacy

69   CHAPTER 5
Integrating Safety into Your Practice

88   CHAPTER 6
Researching Safety Concerns

99   CHAPTER 7
Tech for Vulnerable Groups

110   CHAPTER 8
Proactive Support and Future Work

124   *Conclusion*

126   *Acknowledgments*

129   *Resources*

135   *References*

141   *Index*

*I begin this book by acknowledging the land on which it was written: the traditional and unceded land of the Kiikaapoi (Kickapoo), Peoria, Bodéwadmiakiwen (Potawatomi), Myaamia, and Očhéthi Šakówiŋ peoples.*

*To all the survivors of domestic violence who shared their stories with me, thank you. This book is for you.*

*For Guadalupe Flores, who in 2015 helped the office manager of a nonprofit fix the copy machine and suggested she consider a career in tech.*

# FOREWORD

AS TECHNOLOGISTS, WE TEND to be optimistic. We create products we hope will be experienced in ideal circumstances, in an ideal world, full of ideal users. In reality, we know the world is messy and complicated. But when we reduce human beings simply to "users" in our systems, it's easy to lose sight of the fact that many of them live with systemic oppression, inequity, and interpersonal violence. It's harder still to consider how the products we build can be used to perpetuate these injustices.

As we design and build products, we bring our own priorities, biases, and experiences of the world with us, whether consciously or subconsciously. When we acknowledge this, we find a more nuanced understanding of usability—one that embodies aesthetics and ethics.

What is possible if we embrace this idea? Will the products we build compound the indignities of our messy world, or help us rectify them? Can we address and reduce the potential harms enabled by our systems? And where do we even start?

This book guides us toward urgently-needed answers. In a culmination of years of work, Eva offers a succinct, practical framework for uncovering and mitigating abuse cases. Instead of a vague call to merely consider the harassment, gaslighting, and threats to personal safety our users experience through their devices, she provides a solid set of tools for doing thoughtful, preventative work. Read this book and you'll walk away with a clear strategy for combating tech-facilitated harm.

**—Coraline Ada Ehmke**

# ABOUT THIS BOOK

THIS BOOK DIRECTLY REFERENCES domestic violence, sexual assault, elder abuse, and child abuse.

The stories in this book are stitched together from interviews I conducted with survivors between 2018 and 2020, as well as details from news articles and academic studies.

When relevant, I've added details from my own experiences with technology and design. I've combined details from multiple people's stories to protect the privacy of the dozens of survivors who have so graciously shared their experiences with me. A few of the stories are from friends whose real names I use with permission; all other names are changed.

I had the content reviewed by experts in the support realm to ensure that this book doesn't help abusers find new ways to enact abuse. The reality is that someone intent on abuse is already constantly identifying new methods, and they don't need resources like this one to find them.

## Language and terms

Following is a very short glossary of commonly used terms in this book:

### Domestic violence and intimate partner violence

*Domestic violence* refers to physical, sexual, psychological, emotional, financial, and technological abuse at the hands of a domestic relation. That means abuse from anyone who lives in the home (domestic space): an intimate partner, parent, child, relative, or roommate.

*Intimate partner violence* refers to violence and abuse specifically at the hands of an intimate partner. In the United States, many people use the terms interchangeably, with "domestic violence" often indicating intimate partner violence. I will do the same throughout this book, as many of the examples of technology-facilitated abuse are focused on intimate partners but can also be carried out by other people in the same domestic space.

Domestic and intimate partner violence spans every demographic imaginable. It's a common misconception that domestic violence is limited to people who are poor and uneducated. This could not be further from the truth. Domestic violence occurs in all racial groups; in straight and queer relationships; among teenagers, the elderly, and everyone in between; and among people of all income and education levels.

## Gaslighting

*Gaslighting* is a form of psychological abuse where victims are given false information that leads them to question their sanity and ability to tell fact from fiction. People subjected to gaslighting often question their own memories and feel confused and unable to trust themselves. Abusers who gaslight typically do so with the goal that their victim will only trust the abuser's version of reality rather than their own. Modern tech offers ample opportunities for gaslighting.

## Technology-facilitated domestic violence

*Technology-facilitated domestic violence,* or TFDV, is domestic violence carried out through technology. This area of study is still new, and there are various terms used in this space, such as *technology-facilitated coercive control* and *tech abuse.*

## Victim vs. survivor

Many in the domestic violence and sexual assault advocacy space prefer to use the term *survivor* rather than *victim* for someone who has survived the difficult, dangerous experiences of abuse and assault. *Survivor* centers the person who survived the experience, whereas *victim* places that person in relationship to the abuser. I prefer *survivor* and only use *victim* where it makes sense for clarity or when referring to those who did not survive.

**Technologist**

It gets a bit tiring to continually say "designers, developers, data scientists, project managers, and all the other people who influence how technology is designed and built." So I use the term *technologist* to encapsulate this group.

## What we'll cover in this book

This book tackles the various ways people weaponize everyday technology for harm against others in their lives and how we can combat this harm. The focus is on *interpersonal* harm: the ways users utilize our products to control, abuse, and stalk people in their lives (as opposed to more global and anonymous problems with technology, such as the spread of misinformation).

Gendered abuse related to digital media (harassment on social media platforms, threatening messages, impersonating a partner, and sharing sexual content without consent) is covered at length in other books and articles. I've provided sources so you can learn more about these issues in the Resources section at the end.

# INTRODUCTION

WHEN WE CREATE a new app or design a new feature, we rarely question whether the product we're working on is inadvertently reproducing violent forms of oppression. Most of us were never taught to ask, "Could someone use this product to harm someone else?"

But we should. Although technology plays an intimate role in our lives, it typically ignores the more difficult and tragic realities of what those intimate lives can look like. In the United States, one in three women and one in four men have experienced violence from an intimate partner—potentially over 30 percent of our users (http://bkaprt.com/dfs37/00-01, PDF). And some of that abuse is being enabled, sometimes even tacitly encouraged, by the technology we build.

As technologists, we often think about our users in terms of idealized interactions with our products. And while there's been a shift toward designing in ways that are more accessible and inclusive, our training rarely teaches us to look for differences in users' power and privilege or to examine how those factors play out in an intimate setting.

The sad truth is that the people we are most closely connected to—our families, friends, and especially our significant others—can be controlling, abusive, and eager to turn personal and household tech against us. As designers, we need to consider this threat model in the work we do.

*Designing for safety* means realistically assessing how technological products will be used for harm, prioritizing the prevention of that harm, and giving power and agency to the most vulnerable users: those experiencing domestic violence, people being stalked, sexual assault survivors, the elderly, children, and others whose identities and contexts make them especially at risk of harm. When we fail to explicitly design for groups who may be harmed, we unintentionally prioritize abusers.

Designing for safety also means understanding the root causes of abuse and violence. Our design practice must be grounded in an ongoing, lifelong effort to acknowledge, understand, and dismantle white supremacy, heteropatriarchy, settler colonialism, capitalism, ableism, and other forms of systemic and structural inequality.

A good place to begin is by assuming that some of your users, today, are experiencing abuse. Recent statistics about various types of harm in the US tell a grim story:

Black women experience domestic violence at a disproportionately high rate, but are less likely than white women to be believed by police, jurors, and judges (http://bkaprt.com/dfs37/00-02, PDF).

American Indian and Alaska Native women face domestic abuse at the highest rate of any group, and roughly two thirds of Native women who are sexually assaulted are attacked by non-Native men (http://bkaprt.com/dfs37/00-03, PDF).

The leading cause of death of pregnant people is murder at the hands of a current or former intimate partner (http://bkaprt.com/dfs37/00-04).

One in six women and one in nineteen men have been stalked at some point during their lives (http://bkaprt.com/dfs37/00-05).

At least one out of ten people over the age of sixty are victims of elder abuse (http://bkaprt.com/dfs37/00-06).

It is dangerous to imagine that our users are exempt from violence and abuse. Against this dire backdrop, it's clear that we need to design technology in ways that prevent abuse—and to give power back to survivors facing life-and-death circumstances.

## A path forward

This book is called *Design for Safety*, but it isn't just for people with the title "designer." It's for anyone who influences how technology is made: designers, developers, data scientists, project managers, and everyone in between.

Together, we'll explore what it means to design for safety:

- We'll discuss some of the harmful assumptions about our users that we carry with us into the design process and how we can overcome them.
- We'll look at examples of tech that have been subverted for harm through shared user accounts, internet-connected devices and cars, location-revealing data, and surveillance.
- We'll discuss how to integrate these lessons into your current design practice, including a process to help identify and prevent abuse before it happens, and tactics to help survivors recognize abuse and regain control.
- We'll share best practices for conducting research when designing for safety, especially when working directly with users who may have experienced trauma, and when creating products specifically aimed at vulnerable groups.
- Lastly, we'll zoom out and take a look at the current status of the tech industry, discuss more systemic approaches to problems of technology-facilitated abuse, and explore how we can create a paradigm shift toward safe and ethical tech.

When we put safety at the heart of our process and prioritize the security and well-being of vulnerable users, we end up creating better experiences for everyone. This book will show you how to start doing the important work of designing for safety.

# 1
# OVERCOMING OUR ASSUMPTIONS

GIVING PREFERENCE TO THE RIGHTS of dominant groups is so baked into American society that it's like the air we breathe—difficult for people to recognize as a deliberate choice. And because this silent prioritization is such a common and invisible part of our society, we often reproduce it in the tech we build without even realizing it. It's no coincidence that tech defaults to prioritizing the desires of culturally dominant groups (white, male, able-bodied, cisgender, etc.) unless careful and explicit priority is given to support a marginalized group.

Consider the Amazon Echo's Drop In feature, which allows other Echo users to automatically connect and begin a conversation. The person receiving the communication never gets the option to accept or decline to call—it just starts. Although users can edit who has permission to drop in on them, the privacy issue remains, as people can simply drop in and listen and watch what you're doing at any time. The Echo's design prioritizes the ability to eavesdrop and monitor at the expense of the other users' agency, privacy, and safety (http://bkaprt.com/dfs37/01-01).

Why can't those users just edit their permissions? Well, it's often not that simple in abuse situations, which usually involve a power discrepancy at their core. Elizabeth Yardley, a criminologist who researches gendered violence and homicide, frames the problem as related to many technologists' neoliberal view that "life is a level playing field" in which everyone can self-actualize their way out of harmful interactions. In a blog post expanding on this concept, Yardley writes:

> There is the assumption that the owners and users of online accounts are one and the same, that mutuality and trust exist between people sharing a residence, that end users don't intend to use their tech to do harm and that the main "risks" around technology come from outside of the home from hackers, fraudsters and identity thieves. The fact that women are in more danger from those inside than outside of their homes has not registered with big tech. (http://bkaprt.com/dfs37/01-02)

The Echo is the first of many examples in this book of tech whose design makes dangerous assumptions about its users:

- The drop in feature won't be used for secretly listening to someone without their consent.
- The benefits of convenience outweighed the feature's safety and privacy concerns.

This prioritizes the rights of abusers who misuse the feature for eavesdropping over their victims' right to privacy—a skewed prioritization that we'll see in other examples of personal tech as well.

There are a handful of assumptions that are so deeply held in our overall culture and society that they're tough to recognize as influencing the way we design our tech. To design for safety, we need learn to recognize and work against commonly held assumptions and be able to identify whose rights we're prioritizing and whose rights we're minimizing.

The Echo provides a ready-made feature for secretly listening in on someone without their consent, which is an example of the assumption that is most important for designers to unlearn: the assumption that our users aren't hurting each other with tech.

# PEOPLE HURT EACH OTHER

As designers, we tend to rely on happy but inaccurate assumptions about the close relationships our users have: whether romantic, familial, professional, or platonic, we assume these relationships are composed of people with equal rights within the relationship, who treat each other with care and respect.

This is, as we've seen from the earlier statistics, far from true. The harsh reality is that abuse and violence is a commonplace occurrence within families, friendships, workplaces, and intimate relationships. But this reality isn't accurately reflected in popular culture, the media, or legislation—and we rarely bring it up at work when discussing users or product designs.

Many survivors choose not to disclose their experiences, even to their family or closest friends. Once you or someone very close to you experiences trauma from abuse and/or violence, its prevalence in our wider society becomes obvious; but without at least indirect experience, the pervasiveness of abusive relationships typically remains hidden.

When designing any product or digital experience that will involve couples, families, friends, or workers, we need to dismantle the assumption that these relationships are always healthy. Ours users are people, and many people choose to hurt, or will be hurt by, those who are closest to them. When we start our work from this foundational understanding, we're more likely to prevent users from being harmed by our product or service and better equipped to give support to survivors.

# ABUSERS WILL SUBVERT YOUR PRODUCT

Whatever abuse cases we can identify for our product, abusers will also identify, and more. I'm very intentional about discussing that people *will* abuse our products rather than framing it in terms of what *might* happen. If abuse is possible, it's only a matter of time until it happens. There is no *might*.

"Abusers, stalkers, and other bad actors are going to use any tool they can to control and abuse their victim," says Chris Cox, the executive director of Operation Safe Escape, a nonprofit that helps survivors identify the ways their abuser is digitally tracking and monitoring them, and escape safely (http://bkaprt.com/dfs37/01-03). Abusers are always motivated and are often highly creative about finding new tools for hurting their victims, and tech is not exempt.

Carmen Pitre agrees. She's the president and CEO of the Sojourner Family Peace Center, which provides domestic violence prevention and intervention services, and in an interview in early 2021 explained that she and her colleagues expect abusers to weaponize tech for harm:

> *Anything that technology was designed to do can be used for harmful purposes. The bedrock on which this sits is that abusive relationships are all about control. And anything that an abuser can do to control a victim, he'll do...Abusers are thinking about ways to use whatever tactic they can, including technology. If they're intent on hurting that person, they're already thinking about ways that they can use technology.*

In design terms, it's a guarantee that some of our users will be viewing our product's affordances with a keen eye for how they can use it to further exert power and control over their victim. According to Pitre, "Technology really has expanded the universe for abusers. It blew opportunities for abusers to hurt survivors wide open."

The good news is that technologists have the power to close the door of opportunity that's currently open to abusers, and it starts with recognizing and accepting the guarantee that people will seek to use our specific piece of tech to enact abuse.

## PASSWORDS AREN'T ALWAYS SECRET

Passwords represent the primary (and sometimes only) method of digital account security and privacy. Technologists design account systems under the assumption that passwords are only known and used by the account owner, but this doesn't reflect reality.

Whenever there's a power imbalance in a relationship, the person with more power can simply demand passwords and access their victim's accounts. An abusive spouse might regularly check their partner's browser history. A homophobic parent might monitor their child's social media messages. A manager might read a direct report's emails.

While some abusers may look through their victims' devices secretly, many do so openly. Additionally, someone with access to another person's phone can weaponize various apps for monitoring and stalking by adding themselves as a user or by sharing the victim's location with their own phone (a form of tech-facilitated abuse that we'll discuss in Chapter 3).

Once we upend the assumption that the only threats to account security are malicious hackers, data breaches, and phishing scams, we're better positioned to design safeguards into our products so that users can quickly understand when an abuser has infiltrated their accounts.

## CONSENT IS NOT A GIVEN

We often assume that the people using our products have consented to using our product or a specific feature. If the piece of tech lives on their device and they're the ones who created the account, why would we think otherwise? But this is not always the case.

One example is location-sharing features: if a user has shared their location with someone, we assume that they meant to do so and are aware of its functionality and effects. We don't typically incorporate abuse cases into our design strategy, such as when an abuser surreptitiously accesses a user's phone and shares its location with their own phone.

Consent is a theme that will recur over and over again throughout this book, as there are many examples of tech-facilitated abuse that are enabled through issues of assuming consent. We must not expect that our users have consciously consented to using certain features, that they clearly understand exactly how a feature is currently being used, or that they have the tech literacy to undo the action in question.

# CONSENT IS NOT A CONSTANT

Just as consent isn't a given, it's also not a constant. The typical arc of domestic abuse involves the abuser gaining trust in the beginning stages in order to ingratiate themselves into their victim's lives, and slowly increasing power and control as time goes on. This means that while it may have been safe at one point in time to share one's location or add a user to an account, such actions may no longer be safe later if the relationship changes.

With enough time, users may not remember what functionality or sharing they consented to originally, and without reminders, may never recall these past actions. And sometimes when people do remember, they may not know how to modify the settings to increase their safety—for instance, removing the access of a former partner who continues to control a smart home device from afar for harassment or surveillance.

Apple's Find My (previously called Find My iPhone) has a feature for notifying users when someone else leaves or arrives at certain locations, such as a child arriving at school or a spouse leaving work (**FIG 1**). This feature sends an initial notification to the person being tracked, which would seem to alert them to the potential abuse—until we consider that abusers often have access to their victims' phones and can easily delete the single alert to cover their tracks. A safer design would send alerts asking for consent at regular intervals to give survivors more opportunity to realize their location is being monitored in this way and regain control.

A healthy standard of consent I'd like to see more technologists borrow comes from anti-sexual assault practices, which emphasize that consent given in the past does not equal consent in the present moment (http://bkaprt.com/dfs37/01-05). We should ask for consent from our users both at the beginning of certain interactions and at regular intervals of use.

**Get notifications when they've left or arrived.**

You can set up notifications for when friends and family leave or arrive at a place. They'll be notified when you set it up, so no one's privacy is compromised. You can also receive alerts and notifications when your child has arrived at or departed from school.

**FIG 1:** While it's good that Find My sends a notification to a user that someone else will be notified when they've arrived or left a certain location, just one notification isn't enough to truly ensure that no one's privacy is compromised (http://bkaprt.com/dfs37/01-04).

## SURVEILLANCE IS UNETHICAL

We need to push back against the assumption that technology that enables surveillance can be used safely or ethically. There are very few cases where secretly monitoring the digital activities of others is safe or ethical, despite how common both mass surveillance and the more intimate surveillance among family and significant others has become.

Exceptions to this rule are extreme: it may be ethical to temporarily covertly monitor the activity of someone who is suicidal or involved in dangerous activities, but even these situations are complex and require input from experts. What's not complex is that surveillance, both open and covert, has been normalized in our society—to the point that we'll willingly share Ring outtakes as entertainment (http://bkaprt.com/dfs37/01-06, video).

Abusers will readily use surveillance products to secretly monitor their partners, which is invasive at best and can have deadly consequences when they discover their victim is attempting to escape. NPR found that 85 percent of shelters they surveyed were helping survivors whose abusers were monitoring their activity and location through technology (http://bkaprt.com/dfs37/01-07). When we consider the most threatening implications of surveillance for users in vulnerable and dangerous situations, we can better focus on designing for privacy and safety.

We'll discuss the growing normalization of surveillance and stalkerware more in Chapter 4, but for now, we can start from a place of assuming that surveillance is unsafe and unethical rather than from a mindset that it's a benign industry standard.

## CUSTOMERS NEED SUPPORT

I recently heard from a survivor whose abusive partner had locked her out of her Nest thermostat—and she couldn't find a way to talk to someone at Nest to help her regain control. Similarly, a friend of mine has been unable to find any customer service number, email, or chat feature to contact Tesla so she can get her husband added as a full user to the car maker's app. And Airbnb is notorious for making it difficult to contact a real person that the stories of frustrated hosts and guests attempting to resolve issues through chatbots and automated email replies are documented on the website Airbnb Hell (http://bkaprt.com/dfs37/01-08).

Any product capable of harm (which may be "any product," full stop) needs to staff a customer support line where actual humans are trained to listen for both expressed and unexpressed issues in real time. Too many technology companies seem to operate under the assumption that for one reason or another, this level of customer support isn't warranted. Maybe they believe their product is so well designed that no customers will need the support, or maybe they've made a financial decision to eliminate staffing.

At its least harmful, a lack of customer service results in frustrated users; at its most harmful, it can be a literal matter of life and death. Our users deserve access to quality customer service, regardless of the product or their circumstances in using it.

### Tech literacy is a spectrum

For those of us who work in tech, it's easy to forget that the average person doesn't have a high level of tech literacy. This is especially important in the context of interpersonal harm, where an abuser with a high level of tech literacy will weaponize that knowledge against a survivor who has a lower level of tech know-how. We can't assume that users will quickly or easily grasp how our products work.

The same is true when we build safeguards into our tech to help survivors understand how the abuse is happening and make it stop. These aren't power users; they may be using our apps or services for the very first time, and likely while stressed. If we always design for users who have a low level of tech literacy, our tech will be more likely to empower than overwhelm them.

## IMPACT MATTERS MORE THAN INTENT

Often, the harmful impact of technology begins with our own unexamined beliefs, which makes it incredibly important to do the hard work of unlearning our biases and challenging commonly held assumptions about users.

The concept of "impact over intent" means that the actual impact of our actions is more important that whatever our intentions were. We rarely *intend* to cause harm, but harm happens regardless. We don't get a free pass from this reality when we act on assumptions we don't know we have.

It's human nature to want our intentions to be considered in the aftermath of unintentionally hurting someone. But when it comes to the tech we design, intent is irrelevant, and impact is everything.

In the following chapters, we'll dig into the dangerous effects our designs can have when we let assumptions guide us and don't prioritize the impact of tech in our user's lives.

# 2

# WHO'S IN CONTROL?

LISA AND BEN HAVE BEEN married for a year. Things have been bumpy between them for the past few months, with Ben constantly haranguing Lisa about spending too much time with her friends ("Didn't you just get brunch last weekend?") and complaining about how she doesn't walk their dog until it's dark outside ("I work until eight, hon," she protests).

Ben took pains to outfit their apartment with a number of smart devices, including a Nest thermostat and fully connected audio system that he discourages Lisa from using. ("You won't understand it.") Because of this, it's a surprise to Lisa that he's the one who suggests moving out temporarily to get some space—but she agrees to the separation, privately relieved to have a break from his constant criticism.

The first two days are peaceful. On the third day, Lisa comes home from work, and the apartment feels stifling; the poor dog is panting heavily and nearly out of water. Lisa checks the thermostat and is horrified to see it set to 90 degrees Fahrenheit. She adjusts the Nest, opens the windows, and sleeps uneasily that night. How had she missed that?

The same thing happens the next evening. And the next. Lisa looks up Nest support documentation but doesn't see anything matching her situation. No one else she knows has one of these things, and she's worried about hurting the dog. Reluctantly she texts Ben. "Is there some setting I need to know about the Nest? It's been freaking out." Ben's reply is smug: "So now you want me to come back home? I knew you wouldn't last long."

Lisa's confusing and unnerving experience carries the hallmarks of tech abuse used to gaslight victims. Survivors coming from similar situations to Lisa's have reported their abusers using tactics like changing the temperature, blasting music, or switching lights on and off—all remotely, so their victims can't be sure about the reason for the chaos and sometimes begin to doubt their own sanity. In this chapter, we'll look at this phenomenon more closely and identify how safety-minded design could protect people like Lisa from this form of abuse.

## A NEW FRONTIER IN HARM

The modern landscape of internet-connected smart devices offers abusers a multitude of channels to enact control through covert surveillance, stalking, and psychological abuse such as terrorizing and gaslighting. As of 2021, over 40 percent of American homes had at least one smart device, and usage is projected to increase (http://bkaprt.com/dfs37/02-01).

A 2018 *New York Times* report found that the growing presence of smart devices has been accompanied by an increase in people using them for abuse and control, with workers at domestic violence helplines reporting a significant surge in calls about smart home devices. The article also noted that judges who issue restraining orders may need to begin explicitly mentioning use of these smart devices as falling within the realm of "contact," because otherwise, the abuse often continues even after a restraining order is in place (http://bkaprt.com/dfs37/02-02).

While internet-connected devices like Nest thermostats are among the newest methods for abusers to control their significant others, other forms of tech enable domineering behavior as well. In 2014, NPR surveyed over seventy shelters to understand how abusers utilize smartphones and GPS in their abuse. Their research revealed that 85 percent of shelters were working with clients whose abusers tracked them with GPS, and 75 percent had clients whose abusers used in-home security cameras or other listening devices to eavesdrop on their conversations remotely. In an article summarizing the research, Cindy Southworth, who runs the Technology Safety project out of the National Network to End Domestic Violence, explained that "complete and utter domination and control of their victims" is the ultimate goal of abusers:

> [I]t's not enough that they just monitor the victim. They will then taunt or challenge them and say, "Why were you telling your therapist this?" Or "why did you tell your sister that?" Or "why did you go to the mall today when I told you you couldn't leave the house?" (http://bkaprt.com/dfs37/01-07)

As abuse via smart devices and other tech increases, it's urgent that technologists understand the ways that various forms of connectivity can be weaponized for abuse. We have the potential to help vulnerable users and prevent an enormous amount of harm by asking ourselves: "Who's in control?"

## REMOTE HARASSMENT

Researchers have only recently begun to study coercive control via connected devices; unlike more traditional forms of abuse, we do not yet know exactly how widespread the problem is. Our current knowledge comes from firsthand accounts of survivors and those in the domestic violence support space. These accounts show us that the impact of abuse via connected devices is severe:

- A social worker described helping women whose partners locked them inside their own homes using smart locks and also recalled assisting with a woman whose partner would "control the temperatures so it would be hot one minute and freezing the next." Another survivor told interviewers that when her boyfriend was away from their home, he'd terrorize her by remotely activating smart devices in the middle of the night to blast music, turn on the TV, and flicker the lights (http://bkaprt.com/dfs37/02-03).

- An attorney described an abuser who would remotely unlock a survivor's car doors, then, during a custody hearing, blame the survivor for endangering their children (http://bkaprt.com/dfs37/02-04).

- In 2016, Chrysler recalled over a million of their vehicles after a pair of hackers demonstrated to *Wired* magazine that they could remotely take control of an internet-connected 2014 Jeep Cherokee, cutting the transmission while their friend drove it on the highway (the friend was in on this, and it was all done very safely) (http://bkaprt.com/dfs37/02-05). The actions they could have taken, but didn't, included remotely forcing the car to accelerate and slamming the car's breaks, as well as suddenly turning the steering wheel at any speed.

The remote nature of abuse via connected devices is insidious: it allows abusers and other bad actors to do harm from afar, often in a manner that gives the survivor little ability to understand how the abuse is happening or take back control. However, this doesn't mean that connected tech can't be reformed. As designers, we can use multiple methods to both prevent abuse and help survivors regain power and control.

## Add in speed bumps

A very general method for preventing remote harassment is to recognize when it may be occurring and design a speed bump to slow the user down. For example, if a thermostat's settings are constantly being switched between heating and air-conditioning over a short period of time by a user in the home and a user outside the home, the app might send a message to the user outside the home to ask, "Are you sure? It looks like someone who's home wants a different temperature."

While I don't believe that a feature like this would prevent abuse, it might help to reduce it when used together with other solutions. Putting up this sort of roadblock was shown to decrease bullying in an experiment run by an Illinois teenager, who designed a social media feature that would ask the user if they were sure they wanted to post text that had certain bullying-associated keywords in it. Among users who received the alert asking them to reflect before posting something that might be hurtful, there was a 93 percent reduction in abusive posts (http://bkaprt.com/dfs37/02-06).

An alternative to asking the user to reconsider their behavior is to ask if there's some kind of problem. Perhaps there's no control struggle going on, and the device is actually malfunctioning; this would be a way to allow the user to report a legitimate issue. And if the user's intentions are indeed malicious, this speed bump still offers an opportunity to reconsider their actions before doing harm.

In fact, it's not only matters of interpersonal safety that can benefit from an experience that's deliberately slower. Content strategist Margot Bloomstein has written and talked about how intentionally slowing down an online commercial transaction can give customers the time they need to absorb information related to their purchase—resulting in a higher degree of confidence that they've bought the right thing (http://bkaprt.com/dfs37/02-07).

These sorts of roadblocks can also completely block the action from being possible at all. For example, a smart car could recognize that the car is currently in use and prevent a user who is far away from it from remotely unlocking the car doors or taking other actions to control the car.

Use these ideas as a jumping-off point to consider within your own products. How might you design a small barrier that can recognize activity that's indicative of malfunction, user error, or attempt at abuse? Based on the product and its specific potential for harm, you might deliberately slow the user down, ask them to reconsider their action, or even prevent an activity from being possible during certain situations.

## Flag activity that indicates abuse

Digital financial products offer a clear example of tech that is rife with control issues between users. According to The National Network to End Domestic Violence (NNEDV), 99 percent of intimate partner violence cases involve financial abuse (http://bkaprt.com/dfs37/02-08). NNEDV also notes that financial abuse is among the most powerful methods abusers have to keep their victim in the relationship and that it's often a key barrier to a survivor's ability to stay safe when they leave.

Financial abuse is also widespread outside of intimate partner contexts; financial abuse of the elderly is common, and some parents take advantage of their teenage and young adult children's inexperience to steal or control their money. This means that the space of digital banking and other finance-related tech has an enormous opportunity to both help prevent abusers from taking control of another person's finances and to recognize that abuse is possibly happening, which could be easily done using the already-existing tools banks use to identify potential fraud.

For example, credit card companies will commonly flag activities such as a large purchase (like a new refrigerator or speedboat) that seems unusual. This same technology could be used to flag an account that suddenly runs up a large amount of debt, which is a common tactic of abusers; the goal is to ruin the survivor's credit to make them more financially dependent on the abuser. Another method for ruining a survivor's credit score is putting bills in their name and then refusing to pay them; and while there are many reasons someone may not be paying a bill, this is an activity that should be flagged as potentially involving an element of financial abuse.

Once potential abuse has been identified, financial institutions are in a key position to give appropriate support. What counts as "appropriate" will vary, but considering banks usually have robust customer service teams, human-to-human support is well within the realm of possibility. Utility companies should also consider the possibility of financial abuse when working with customers who haven't paid their bills and start with the assumption that the customer may not actually have full control over and access to their finances.

Flagging potentially abusive behavior is possible in other realms as well. Whatever your product, try to identify if there is any behavior that might indicate abuse, and create a design to assist users who may need help. We'll get more into the nuts and bolts of how to do this in Chapter 5.

## ACCOUNT OWNERSHIP

Joint and shared accounts are teeming with struggles over who gets control, and once again, the space of digital personal finance is a prime example. While banks vary on how they handle joint accounts, many are not truly joint accounts at all: they are standard, single-user accounts, modified to allow multiple logins to access them. This means that somewhere in the backend, the account is designed for just one user to have ultimate control. The separate logins aren't truly separate, and the account isn't truly joint: it's an account for one person masquerading as something else.

My husband and I set up our joint bank account in person at a local branch, where the banker who helped us set my husband as the primary user—without telling us. This means when I'm prompted to answer the account's security questions for verification, such as when I log in from a new Wi-Fi network, the questions are based on my husband's information (**FIG 2.1**). This gives him a lot more control over the account, as he can deny me access by not providing the answers.

Later on, I opened a new shared account for us on our bank's website. This time, I was presented with a form that let me set myself as the source of the security quiz questions (**FIG 2.2**). While I was happy that this account would use my information, it doesn't solve the problem; it only shifts the control from my husband to me. The only thing to prevent me from restricting his access to the account are my own ethics, not the system's design.

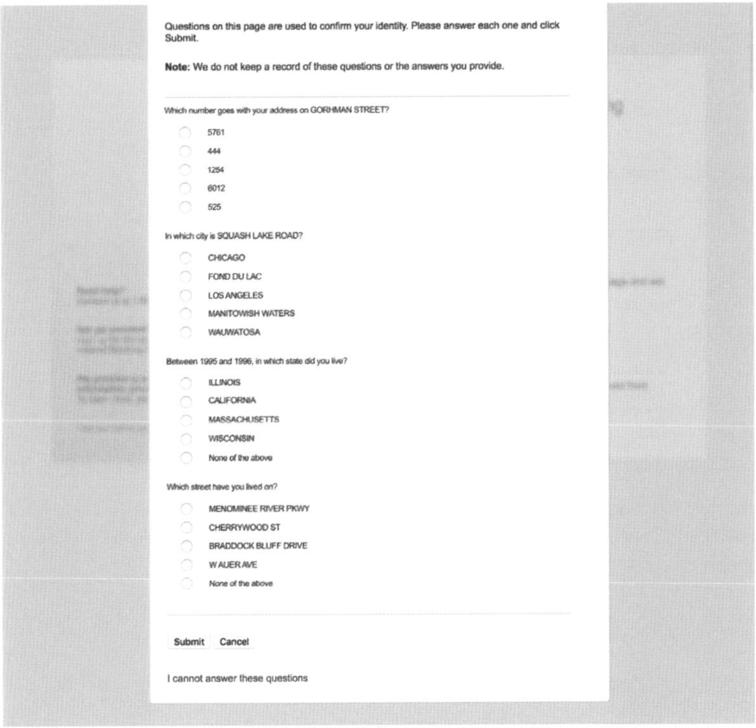

**FIG 2.1:** I have to answer security questions (edited for privacy) about my husband when logging into our joint account from a new Wi-Fi network. Even though I've known him since college, I can only answer half of these questions.

Single-user accounts masquerading as joint accounts aren't restricted to banks. This same problem crops up in many apps and services, from cars to grocery stores to phones, where users might assume an account accessed by two people is jointly controlled.

Ensuring shared control and power in online banking tools and other financial tech is key in preventing financial domestic abuse and adequately responding to users who are experiencing it. Most financial institutions are large, slow to change, and operating under numerous laws and regulations, but change is absolutely possible.

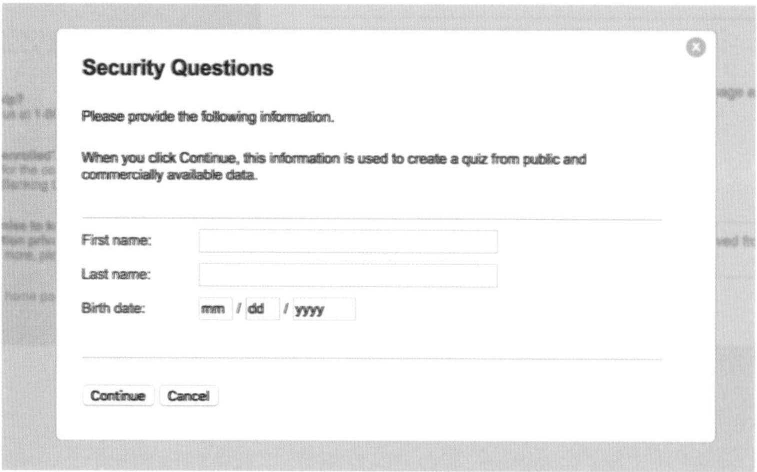

**Security Questions**

Please provide the following information.

When you click Continue, this information is used to create a quiz from public and commercially available data.

First name:

Last name:

Birth date: mm / dd / yyyy

Continue   Cancel

**FIG 2.2:** This account will use my information to generate the security quiz—meaning that now it's my husband whose ability to access the account could be compromised by me simply refusing to give him the answers.

## Create truly joint accounts

For power to be truly shared, each member on an account must have their own login with their own username and password. Identity verification information must then be tied to the individual.

AT&T does a good job of authentically separating out the user identities of two people with a shared account. Instead of a security quiz drawn from publicly available information, they use two-factor authentication by sending a code via text message. When my AT&T account wanted to verify my identity, it presented both my phone number and my husband's. This ensures equal access rather than prioritizing one user over another (**FIG 2.3**).

True joint account ownership also benefits circumstances that have nothing to do with abuse. When interviewing people about their experience with joint bank accounts, I spoke with a man whose wife had passed away several years prior. She had been set as the primary user of their bank account, and

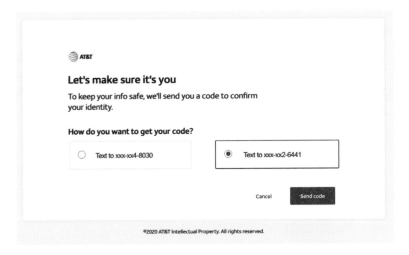

**FIG 2.3:** By supporting multiple phone numbers for verification texts, AT&T ensures two users on an account have equal access.

it took him over a year to gain full access. Similarly, although my grandmother had given my father full control over all of her finances and marked him as her beneficiary, transferring funds and closing her accounts after she died was still a tedious, time-consuming, and months-long process.

A lack of planning by tech companies for life events that separate people—including breakups, moving out of the parent's home, and the death of a family member—is a theme that we'll see again in this book, along with the idea that when we put safety at the heart of our design, we end up creating a better, more inclusive experience for all our users.

## Be transparent about who's in control

My friends Claudia and Mark live in Chicago, and like many people in big cities, both use public transportation to commute to work and only need one car.

Mark had wanted a Tesla Model 3 for ages, and finally, when their old car was on its last legs, Claudia agreed to the purchase.

They sat down together with her iPad and paid the $100 deposit to reserve their car.

Several months later, when they received their shiny new car, they realized that the digital account tied to Tesla's app had been created completely in Claudia's name. While the title of the car had both their names on it, and legally they both own it, Claudia is the sole digital owner in Tesla's eyes. This means she has access to the full set of features, such as setting a maximum speed and adding others to the app, while Mark is merely a "Driver," invited to the account by Claudia. She can remove him from the account with a tap of a finger, which would also remove his ability to access the car itself. There is no way to create a second primary user. Unlike the joint bank account, which sneakily creates a primary and secondary user while pretending all users are the same, the design of the Tesla app accounts forces users into primary and secondary users, without making it clear up front how the division takes place.

When Claudia and Mark reserved their Model 3, they had no idea that their casual decision to make the payment from Claudia's iPad, which was tied to her Apple Pay account, would be interpreted as authorization to make her the primary user of the car. A better design would have made this clear; a safer design still would allow them to create two primary users and have an authentically joint account. Just like with the joint bank accounts, control is being given to one person in an opaque way.

In an abusive scenario, where Claudia would use this as a form of control over Mark, a design that made it clear how much control Claudia had over the car would give Mark important information about his safety when driving it.

## Allow users to "split" accounts

A potential solution to Claudia and Mark's dilemma is to allow Mark to "detach" his accounts away from Claudia's and into a new one that has full permissions. In a personal conversation, sociologist and software tester Jorunn Mjøs suggested a feature to "clone" (or copy) an existing account as the basis for a new one as well as the ability to "detach" an individual profile and use it to create a new account. Mjøs's version of "who's in control?" is "who gets custody of the algorithm?"

On streaming services such as Spotify and Netflix, the desire for this sort of feature abounds among users who have a profile on a primary user's account and want to create a new one for themselves while keeping the data from their previous profile. People want (and regularly ask for) this feature for all sorts of reasons, including breakups, moving away from parents or roommates, and being in a place where they can finally afford their own account. Instead, secondary users are left with no options but to start over, while the account holder, or primary user, gets to keep their profile as well as the wealth of data, which is often built up over years and typically includes precise recommendations.

The concept of cloning or detaching a profile and spinning it into a new account is technically complex but by no means impossible and would enable users to turn one account into two, which translates to a new user who already understands the product and is a loyal customer. This is another example of how focusing on designing for safety would make a product better for people in all sorts of situations. For products like the Tesla, which was initially designed for a single primary user, allowing secondary users like Mark to detach his profile and use it to create a primary user profile may be a possible retrofitted solution.

## Give customers proper support

It may legitimately not be possible to design a piece of tech in a way that ensures two people get equal control, and your stakeholder may choose to proceed anyway. When this is the case, it is especially important to ensure that there's a way to talk to a real human at the company. Someone who has the knowledge necessary to help people who are being abused by their product, whether it's a Tesla user being denied access to the car or someone whose finances are being controlled by an abusive partner.

Claudia and Mark searched for a way to get in touch with someone at Tesla, but "contact us" forms seemed to go nowhere, and they were unable to reach a human being who might be able to make Mark the primary user of their Tesla. In an abusive situation, this would quickly put Mark in danger, as he would have no way to use the car without Claudia knowing. This is why self-serve forms can't replace human interactions in a way that supports user safety.

For an example of what enhanced support looks like, we can look to two major banks in Australia, the National Australia Bank and the Commonwealth Bank of Australia, who have created hotlines staffed with specially trained employees to assist customers experiencing domestic abuse. The Australian Banking Association set a goal to "minimize the burden" on customers affected by domestic violence by:

- creating guidelines for bank staff that include ensuring the customer's contact information is kept private from a joint account holder,
- providing copies of documents without a fee, and
- referring customers who want additional help to a local domestic violence organization (http://bkaprt.com/dfs37/02-09).

The hotlines were so popular during the pilot phase that they have become a permanent part of the banks' overall customer support ecosystem. Banks in other countries, as well as other companies in general, would do well to follow the model of providing customer support specifically to vulnerable user groups. Services like this can help victims of financial abuse quickly regain control over their money and begin to rebuild their financial health, decreasing reliance on an abuser and helping them leave dangerous situations more quickly and safely.

At the end of the day, giving users the ability to get in touch with a human being who can understand complex human situations is essential to both a quality customer experience and to preventing abuse.

## DIGITAL VS. PHYSICAL CONTROL

When asking "who's in control" of a piece of tech we're designing, there are certain scenarios where we should also ask ourselves if digitizing control is the right move in the first place. Sometimes, the fact that we *can* digitize an analog product doesn't necessarily mean we *should*.

Examples abound of connected digital devices presenting frustrating problems that range from the trivial to the serious. A roundup from the Twitter account Internet of Shit (http://bkaprt.com/dfs37/02-10) in late 2020 included gems like:

- internet-connected shoes automatically connecting to their owner's headphones,
- a couple who changed internet routers and can no longer connect their living room's smart lightbulbs ("It's literally been dark in there for months now"), and
- a smart doorbell on a residence inexplicably displaying the booking website for a British hotel, making the doorbell unusable.

And in early 2021, an internet-connected sex toy made headlines when hackers exploited a security vulnerability to lock the devices, demanding ransom before giving back control:

*[S]ecurity researchers found that the manufacturer of an Internet of Things chastity cage—a sex toy that users put around their penis to prevent erections that is used in the BDSM community and can be unlocked remotely—had left an API exposed, giving malicious hackers a chance to take control of the devices. That's exactly what happened. (http://bkaprt.com/dfs37/02-11)*

Luckily, the user who spoke to the press about the hack wasn't wearing the device at the time, but if he had been, the physical implications could have been serious.

In an anecdote my editor told me, a driver found himself unable to drive his Tesla after upgrading his phone, as the car provides few physical fallbacks when the app isn't functional. In another example, a friend recently told me about a problem with a hybrid car she rented: the battery died, and because the locks were fully digital, she wasn't able to open the car door. She was lucky to have been in a location where she had cell service and enough power on her phone to stream a video on YouTube that showed her how to access a hidden keyhole to get into the car. This happened to her while alone in a new city on a freezing winter day, which could have meant more trouble.

Digitized control can abruptly turn into "no control" when conditions shift, which is frustrating in best-case scenarios and life-threatening in others. A car can be a literal lifeline to people in domestic violence situations; they are often an instrumental part of survivors' escape plans. Currently, many cars still operate with a key that opens the doors, but Tesla has migrated most of its controls (including locking and unlocking) over to their app. The company does provide a credit card-like key card meant for valets that can be used as a physical key in a pinch, but this does not solve the problem of a primary user being able to digitally restrict a partner's access to the car. In cases where an abuser is the "primary" person with full digital control over the vehicle, survivors face an even larger hurdle if they are attempting to leave the relationship.

Smart locks pose the even more dire risk of denying people access to their own homes. Many landlords are switching from traditional keys to smart locks in order to have easier control over who has building access and to reduce headaches when tenants lose physical keys; but not all tenants share their enthusiasm. Apps associated with smart locks can come along with aggressive data collection, including collecting GPS information. With the heightened potential for privacy violations, smart lock systems make it easier for landlords to force evictions, particularly of lower-income tenants who are unlikely to be able to afford an attorney to fight back (http://bkaprt.com/dfs37/02-12).

In Brooklyn, tenants of a rent-controlled building organized against their landlord's use of internet-connected entry system software that used AI facial recognition, pointing out issues with privacy as well as the overwhelming evidence that AI systems are less accurate when it comes to recognizing the faces of Black people, which could lead to them being locked out of their homes (http://bkaprt.com/dfs37/02-13). This fear is well-founded: a 2019 analysis from the National Institute of Standards and Technology found that top-performing facial recognition systems misidentified Black people at rates five to ten times higher than white people (http://bkaprt.com/dfs37/02-14). (For more on the ways AI and algorithms reproduce racism, see the Resources section.)

### Design physical fallbacks

Just because it's possible to connect something to the internet doesn't always mean we should. When a client or stakeholder insists on doing so anyway, we designers need to ensure there are physical fallbacks—be it a building's front door lock, a home's doorbell, or a chastity cage's ability to open. Users need to be able to regain control when the high-tech elements inevitably fail—or are tampered with by a hostile party.

Be mindful, too, that common scenarios like owners changing their internet password, purchasing a new router, or updating their phone software won't brick the entire system.

## WHO IS THE SOURCE OF TRUTH HERE?

When devices become digitized and internet connected, issues with transparency around the use of the devices often arise as well. Without the ability to "prove" that an abuser who's no longer in the home is remotely manipulating the environment, survivors risk not being believed about their abuse—or worse, deemed to be having hallucinations or a psychotic episode. A domestic violence advocate told the *New York Times* that some of her clients had been put on psychiatric holds to have their mental state evaluated after reporting abuse involving internet of things (IoT) devices (http://bkaprt.com/dfs37/02-02).

Documenting abuse is key to building a case against an abuser, and the way we as technologists can assist in this situation is to put more concrete evidence in survivors' hands. So how do we build better transparency into these smart devices so that abusers' activities are no longer hidden from view?

## Provide history logs

History logs for connected tech, such as smart home devices and connected cars, offer an avenue for survivors to provide proof of their abuse and combat the type of gaslighting that so many abusers specialize in.

Home Assistant provides an excellent example of how history logs can be kept and viewed by users. The software is designed to be the central control system in a home full of various smart devices, managing them all in one place. Its logs track moment-to-moment user actions as well as regularly scheduled actions, such as turning the lights on at the same time each morning (**FIG 2.4**).

Should you have the opportunity to introduce history logs to your product, or improve the logging system that may already be in place, consider these essential elements that can help reduce the power of abusers:

- Ensure the history logs include the username of the person who took the action, what the action was, and the date and time it occurred.
- Make history logs available through both the app and the device itself to account for instances when a victim of abuse through that product doesn't have the app installed.
- Make it clear to users if the logs will not be stored beyond a certain date, as gathering evidence of abuse is important for survivors who engage in the criminal-legal system or have other reasons to want proof of the abuse (such as custody over children). Ideally, history logs would provide data as far back as the device was in use, but a more realistic goal might be to provide history for the previous six months.
- Additionally, you'll want to think carefully about not just how a user can view the history logs but how they can download or record it so they can use it later as proof of the abuse.

**Logbook**

Start date: January 20, 2021, 6:00 PM  End date: January 21, 2021, 9:00 PM  Entity

- Amazon Alexa **send command Alexa.PowerController/TurnOff for Side Lights by Home Assistant Cloud**
  9:42:39 PM · 2 days ago

- Basement Left **turned off by** Basement All Off
  9:34:09 PM · 2 days ago

- Basement Right **turned off by** Basement All Off
  9:34:08 PM · 2 days ago

- Basement All Off **has been triggered by state of light.basement_center**
  9:34:08 PM · 2 days ago

- Basement Center **turned off**
  9:34:08 PM · 2 days ago

- Johnson Home **changed to Partly cloudy**
  9:33:20 PM · 2 days ago

- LG webOS TV 3C46 **changed to problem**
  9:24:17 PM · 2 days ago

- Amazon Alexa **send command Alexa.Discovery/Discover by Home Assistant Cloud**
  8:55:25 PM · 2 days ago

- SarahsAplWatch **was at home**
  8:55:13 PM · 2 days ago

- SarahsAplWatch **was away**
  8:53:38 PM · 2 days ago

- Basement Bedroom **turned off by Owen Johnson**
  8:37:58 PM · 2 days ago

- MDiPad **was at home**
  8:29:40 PM · 2 days ago

FIG 2.4: The Logbook feature of my coworker's Home Assistant gives a thorough history of actions taken, including the time, date, and user who performed the action, which greatly reduces the ability of one user to gaslight another by claiming they didn't use the device.

A number of connected devices reveal some data to the user but not to such a granular level as specific user activity. For example, Nest collects an enormous amount of data from its customers to use in its partnerships with utility companies (http://bkaprt.com/dfs37/02-15). However, the company doesn't share most of this data with its users; perhaps they think no one would want to view a list of all the times someone in their household adjusted the temperature, and at what time, and which user took the action. But if this data were revealed to the user, it would go a long way to help survivors escape gaslighting and make their case to law enforcement. At the bare minimum, users should be able to easily request history logs so that they can increase the chance of their abuse being taken seriously.

## SAFER TECH IS TRANSPARENT

Technology has transformed a plethora of everyday tasks, such as going to the bank, unlocking a door, and starting a car, from in-person analog interactions to high-tech and internet-enabled exchanges. With that change has come a struggle for control over the tech that powers our lives. We must resist privileging the rights of those who would weaponize our tech for abuse. We must instead ask ourselves whose right to control is being enabled—or threatened—with any new piece of tech, and consciously prioritize the rights and safety of our most vulnerable users.

Much of the tech in question is still in a nascent form, meaning we can still course-correct before patterns of harm become the standard. And just because other tech that involves thorny issues of control are more established, such as financial products, doesn't mean they can't be rethought. We have the ability to update long-established norms and retrofit them for safety, such as changing the long tradition of people using technology for stalking—the topic of our next chapter.

# 3 THE DANGERS OF LOCATION-REVEALING DATA

ERIC AND ROB HAD been together about eight months, and Eric was feeling exhausted. Rob had become increasingly fixated on Eric's friendships, twice even accusing him of having an affair. After catching Rob snooping on his phone, again, Eric broke it off. It was like Rob didn't trust him to have a life outside of their relationship.

The very next evening, Eric is at a pub with some friends when he spots Rob, settling into a seat at the other side of the bar. He leaves quickly, chalking it up to a creepy coincidence. But the next day, Eric runs into Rob at the grocery store. Rob doesn't even live in the same neighborhood. The texts begin the next day: "How was Sandwichland?"—the café where Eric had just grabbed lunch with a colleague.

Eric realizes he's being stalked, but he can't figure out how Rob's doing it. Eric is tech-savvy and decides to turn off location services on social media, asks his friends not to post photos that show his location, and double-checks he isn't sharing his location on Google Maps. But Rob continues to show up wherever Eric goes. What did Eric miss? How is Rob still finding him? Becoming more and more scared, Eric begins to turn off his phone whenever he leaves the house, certain that this will put a stop to Rob's knowledge. But the next day, Eric sees Rob walk past the coffee shop he's sitting in.

It's a full month before Eric realizes what's happening. He gets an annoying survey alert from the app he uses to control his car's GPS navigation and sound system, which has way more features than he ever uses. Instead of dismissing the pop-up, Eric opens the app, and his blood runs cold. "Find my car" location tracking is a feature. Rob had installed the app on his phone, too, while they were dating—to control the music, of course, like everything else. Now he was able to see the car's location as well.

Eric had done everything right to try to hide from Rob, but in today's constantly evolving tech landscape, there's always another location-sharing feature around the corner.

## OLD CRIME, NEW TOOLS

Stalking is a crime with serious repercussions. One in six women and one in nineteen men are stalked at some point during their lives, according to the National Coalition Against Domestic Violence, and survivors suffer higher than average rates of depression, anxiety, and insomnia. One in seven survivors of stalking are forced to move, one in eight lose work, and one in four contemplate suicide.

Worst of all, stalking is often a precursor to murder. A study in the *American Journal of Public Health* found stalking to be among the risk factors in abusive relationships that ended in femicide (the murder of the woman in the relationship) (http://bkaprt.com/dfs37/03-01).

Within this context, designers and other technologists have an imperative to take stalking seriously and to be extremely careful with how location-revealing data is used and shared.

Modern tech enables stalking in a multitude of ways. While location-sharing features are among the more straightforward methods that stalkers use to track their victims, there are many more complex, but still highly effective, approaches as well. Modern cars, for example, frequently connect to the internet in order to offer mobile app–friendly digital controls. This design provides ample opportunity for stalking a driver, who often won't realize that someone else is able to view the car's location (http://bkaprt.com/dfs37/03-02).

Cars have played a role in domestic violence for a long time: before the age of digital automobile interfaces, a common tactic was for abusers to check the odometer of the victim's car to see if they had driven any extra miles outside of those necessary to get to work or the grocery store. Once small tracking devices entered the market, it became commonplace for abusers to secretly attach them to their victim's cars so the abuser can stalk them. "These are modern forms of old tactics and behaviors," observed Erica Olsen, director of the Safety Net Project at the National Network to End Domestic Violence. "The behavior is not new, but the technology is" (http://bkaprt.com/dfs37/03-03).

Considering the relationship between stalking and murder, we want tech to help survivors remain hidden, not broadcast their location unprompted. Making it easy to boot out unwanted users and quickly understand and modify privacy settings can be a matter of life and death.

## STALKING BY DEFAULT

In September of 2020, Andrew Seward, head of data product development at Experian, brought to light how fitness app Strava had exposed the location data of a fellow Strava user he passed during a run. This brief moment, too passing to even be described as an authentic encounter, prompted Andrew's Strava app to tag the woman's profile as having made an appearance during his workout (**FIG 3.1**). He was able to click on her photo and see her full name as well as a map of her running routes, which effectively revealed where she lived (http://bkaprt.com/dfs37/03-04).

Seward double-checked that his Strava account wasn't following the woman's (it wasn't), and further investigation revealed that she had even turned off public sharing information—meaning her activity was, theoretically at least, hidden from people whom she had not accepted as followers.

**FIG 3.1:** Andrew Seward's Strava app showing the name of the unknown user he passed by. The app says this user was "with" him on the run, despite Seward not knowing who she is and her profile being set to private. Image courtesy of Andrew Seward.

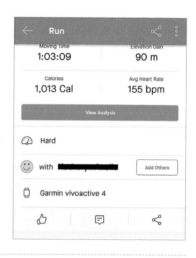

Seward attributed this inadvertent data-sharing to Strava's Flyby feature, which allows the user to "see athletes who were nearby and where you crossed paths." Other Twitter users responding to his tweets put the blame on the Group Activities feature, which groups users who have a certain amount of overlap during their workouts, such as jogging near each other for some amount of time. (How close the users need to be and how long they need to be exercising on the same route is unclear.) At the time of Seward's tweets, both Group Activities and Flyby allowed "Everyone" to view the information by default. (**FIG 3.2**).

Seward's analysis of the safety implications of the Flyby feature continued:

> Worth remembering that someone knowing where you live isn't the only risk, it's not even the biggest risk. It's also knowing the route, knowing where you go that's dark or secluded and at what time, and that it is probably a regular routine. (http://bkaprt.com/dfs37/03-05)

Since Seward's tweets, Strava changed the Flyby feature to be set to "No One" by default, so that users have to opt in to

# Privacy Controls

## Where You Appear

### Profile Page

Your profile page displays information about you, such as your name, activities, followers, photos and stats. Parts of your profile page will always be publicly available. Learn More.

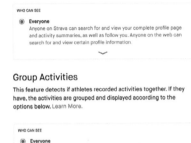

WHO CAN SEE

◉ Everyone
Anyone on Strava can search for and view your complete profile page and activity summaries, as well as follow you. Anyone on the web can search for and view certain profile information.

### Activities

Activities are workouts, races or events you record or upload to Strava. What you choose below will be your **default**, but you can change settings for each individual activity. You will appear in group activities or Flybys unless you adjust those controls. Learn More.

WHO CAN SEE

◉ Everyone
Anyone on Strava can view your activities. Your activities will be visible on segment and challenge leaderboards, and other Strava features.

### Group Activities

This feature detects if athletes recorded activities together. If they have, the activities are grouped and displayed according to the options below. Learn More.

WHO CAN SEE

◉ Everyone
Your group activities will be visible to anyone on Strava.

### Flyby

Flybys provide in-depth activity playbacks to anyone on Strava or the web. Flybys allow you to rewatch any activity minute by minute, and see athletes who were nearby and where you crossed paths. Learn More.

WHO CAN SEE

◉ Everyone
Your activities are accessible to you and anyone on the web using Flybys. Only your activities marked as visible to 'Everyone' will be displayed in Flybys.

**FIG 3.2:** The Group Activities and Flyby features in Andrew Seward's Strava app were set to the most public setting by default, making his information public in a way he never truly consented to.

being tagged as a "flyby" in other user's apps. However, the three other settings under the privacy settings (Profile Page, Activities, and Group Activities) still default to being visible to anyone else on Strava, which is an issue of implied consent. A user who doesn't go into the settings to change them to be private has not actually consented to making their information public. In these features, consent is assumed, rather than asked for and received.

Additionally, while the rest of the settings have three privacy features—Everyone, Followers, and No One—the Flyby feature has only two: Everyone and No One. This means that a user who wants to both enjoy the social factor that Strava offers and stay safe is out of luck; they have to choose either safety or sociability.

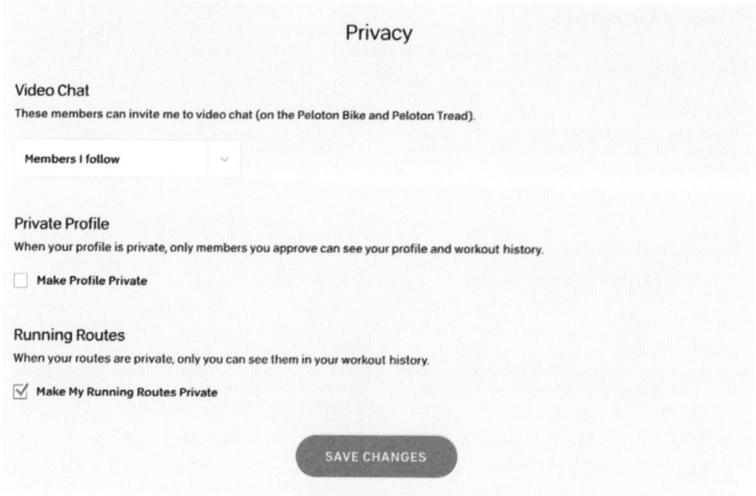

## Privacy

**Video Chat**

These members can invite me to video chat (on the Peloton Bike and Peloton Tread).

| Members I follow | ∨ |
| --- | --- |

**Private Profile**

When your profile is private, only members you approve can see your profile and workout history.

☐ Make Profile Private

**Running Routes**

When your routes are private, only you can see them in your workout history.

☑ Make My Running Routes Private

SAVE CHANGES

**FIG 3.3:** Unlike Strava, Peloton sets its users' running routes to private by default. This allows the user to give proper consent to their location information becoming public.

### Make privacy the default setting

When it comes to any sort of feature that might let others see a user's location, the default should be privacy. Users shouldn't need to understand how to configure these settings out of the box. When privacy is the default and the location hidden from public view, that means the users are protected by default as well.

Strava should take a cue from fitness app Peloton and set all location-revealing features to private until the user chooses to make them public (**FIG 3.3**).

# COVERT MISUSE OF LOCATION-SHARING FEATURES

Location-sharing services such as Google Maps and Apple's Find My are also easy to subvert for stalking and, like the Strava Flyby feature, are dangerous in that they do so without making the user aware of what's going on.

As an experiment, Andy Greenberg, a writer at *Wired*, asked his wife to see if she could find a way to secretly monitor his location using only the apps he already had installed on his phone. Greenberg's wife was able to do so with three apps:

- First was Glimpse, a location-sharing app similar to the location-sharing feature of Google Maps. While using Greenberg's phone, she sent herself a text message with his location, which is how he identified that this was her first method. (A true abuser would likely have deleted that text message from their partner's phone in order to cover their tracks.)
- Next came Google Maps, and Greenberg spent the entire day being tracked by his wife. Only when his battery was low did he open the app, seeing then that his location was shared—the app had not given him any indication that it was being used.
- It was the same the next day with Find My, which gave no warning or indication that his location was being shared (http://bkaprt.com/dfs37/03-06).

Greenberg tested the potential of these apps to be used for stalking with the approach of an experimenter, but there are plenty of real-life examples of abusers engaging in exactly this behavior:

- In 2018, an Australian mechanic stalked and terrorized an ex-girlfriend through an app integrated with her Land Rover. He used her car's registration information to set himself up as an owner of the car and was able to remotely start and stop the car, control its windows, and track its location.

After he was arrested, authorities searching his home found a list of places she frequented and upcoming events she was scheduled to attend, as well as a list of weapons and their costs (http://bkaprt.com/dfs37/03-07).

- A man in England helped his Bumble date locate her iPhone with his Find My app, and later, when she told him she wasn't interested in seeing him again, took advantage of the fact that she hadn't signed out of the app on his phone to stalk and terrorize her (http://bkaprt.com/dfs37/03-08).
- A woman in Illinois with a protective order against her ex-husband was stalked when he obtained their son's iPhone and used the Find My app to track its location, which essentially told him where his ex-wife was. He tracked her location to their daughter's softball game, slashed her car's tires, and was arrested while looking for her. He had forty-seven knives in his car (http://bkaprt.com/dfs37/03-09).
- The online help center for Google Maps includes questions from users about how to prevent stalking and how to ensure that someone has been removed from location sharing. One poster wrote that her stalker was consistently "popping up in the maps app as a suggested person to share my location with," and asked for advice on how to make it stop (http://bkaprt.com/dfs37/03-10).

The problem is not with location-sharing features themselves; it's with the assumption that people sharing locations are always doing so consensually and that the feature is used only within the context of relationships that are equal and trusting. Abuse cases have been left out of the picture entirely. The reality is that many couples know each other's passwords and phone PINs, and within the context of an abusive relationship, designers should assume that the abuser always has access to their victim's phones. Abusers often take advantage of their access to their victim's phone to secretly set up location sharing.

The Share My Location feature in Google Maps allows a user to share their location for set periods: one hour, until the end of the day, or indefinitely. An abuser can simply select the "indefinitely" option, accept the notification on their victim's phone to make it disappear, and then track their victim's location for at

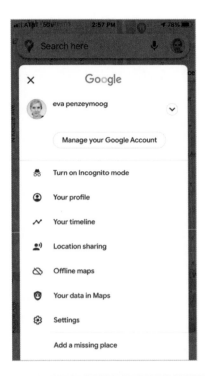

FIG 3.4: The Location Sharing settings in Google Maps are tucked in a menu that loads only upon tapping the user profile picture.

least thirty days without them being any the wiser. Unless the user goes out of their way to check the location-sharing settings, which are somewhat hidden in the Google Maps UI, they won't realize they're sharing their location (FIG 3.4).

## Make location-sharing reminders frequent or persistent

Any location-sharing app or feature should use email or text messages to alert the person whose location has been shared. Google Maps achieves this solution partially by sending an email every thirty days that lists everyone the user is currently sharing their location with (FIG 3.5). While these emails are certainly a massive step in the right direction, a stalker can do a lot of damage in thirty days.

**FIG 3.5:** A monthly summary from Google Maps of who you're sharing your location with is a good start but not enough to ensure safety.

A safer design would frequently and consistently remind users who has access to their location data. For mobile apps, notifications could help. In modern connected cars, the information that the car's location is visible to someone else should be displayed on the car's console when the driver starts the car. This is especially important since the stalking and abuse potentials of modern connected cars are brand new and poorly understood, and often missing from guides to help survivors prevent stalking.

An alternative to frequent reminders about location sharing is to make the information a persistent state. Google Maps itself gives a good example of this sort of design: when the app is being used to give directions between two locations, but the app isn't currently open, a blue bar appears across the top of the

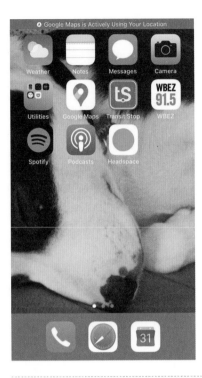

**FIG 3.6:** Google Maps has a persistent bar across the top of the screen when it's using your location, a pattern that could be recreated to ensure users understand who can currently view their location.

phone, alerting the user that the app is using your location (**FIG 3.6**). Using this same design to tell the user that their location is being shared with someone else would greatly reduce the ability of others to secretly monitor the location of another through sharing their location.

## HOW AN EMAIL SERVICE ENABLED STALKING

In the summer of 2019, email client Superhuman came under fire for allowing users in the United States to see not only when their emails had been opened by recipients, but which state those people were in at the time. In response to the privacy controversy that followed, Superhuman CEO Rahul Vohra

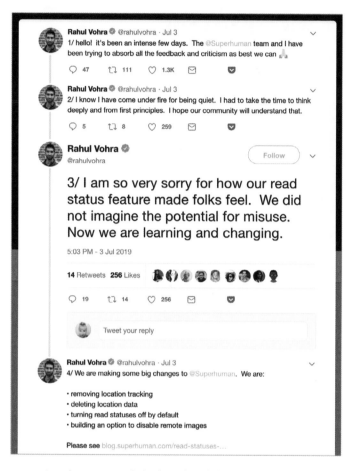

**FIG 3.7:** Superhuman CEO Rahul Vohra acknowledged that he and his team "did not imagine the potential for misuse" before coming under fire for enabling stalking (http://bkaprt.com/dfs37/03-12).

apologized on the company blog and tweeted that the team "did not imagine the potential for misuse" (**FIG 3.7**).

Vohra's blog post indicates that the team had at least some imagination for the potential misuse, however, stating that "we deliberately do not show cities—we only show states or countries" (http://bkaprt.com/dfs37/03-11). Although choosing to show a much broader view of the email recipient's location made the feature a bit safer, the impact could still have been dangerous: for some survivors who have left abusers and worked to keep their new location secret, revealing even the state they're in could have deadly consequences.

One example comes from a friend of mine, Amelia (name changed), who left her abusive girlfriend with the help of Betty, her best friend. Amelia escaped by leaving work in the middle of the day and traveling hundreds of miles out of state to Betty's hometown in Virginia, where she secretly lived with Betty's parents for over a month.

Amelia's abuser knew that Amelia was friendly with Betty's parents and that they were the only people Amelia knew in Virginia. If her abuser had used Superhuman to send Amelia an email, she would have known exactly where she was just through Amelia opening the message. Amelia wouldn't have had to be a Superhuman user herself for her location data to be revealed. She also wouldn't have had to reply to the email. She might have opened it to see if it contained any threatening information or to forward it to a law enforcement agency—and her abuser would have been able to track her down.

Amelia was lucky that her ex didn't use Superhuman or any other tech that so carelessly revealed location data. And just because there aren't any news stories about stalking through Superhuman doesn't mean it didn't happen before the company stopped revealing location data. Thankfully in this case, the CEO didn't feel that "it hasn't happened yet" was a valid reason to not make any changes, but a thorough understanding of the dangers of stalking and designing for safety up front would have been even more ideal.

### Tracking pixels don't ask for consent

Superhuman provided its users with the location data of their email's recipients without getting consent to do so. This should never happen; whenever location data is available—even at a high level, such as the user's state or province—the product must get consent from the user to share it with others. Superhuman accomplished this with the use of tracking pixels, an industry-standard feature for many email clients that's used for marketer-geared metrics like open rates (http://bkaprt.com/dfs37/03-13).

Browser extensions and other products do exist that block tracking pixels, but survivors shouldn't need to be email security experts to protect themselves from this potential abuse case. Superhuman is just another company following the winds of an overall unethical tech ecosystem. We'll spend some time reimagining the field of tech as one that prioritizes ethics and safety in Chapter 8.

**Don't use location data unless it's absolutely necessary**

The potential for harm with location data makes it particularly important to examine the use cases and benefits of collecting such data. There should always be a clear reason for collecting location data, and revealing it should only happen when doing so is key to meeting an important user need.

Many companies choose to collect as much user data as they can, even if they don't have a stated use for that data. We must resist the urge (from both ourselves and our stakeholders) to create features simply because the data to enable it is available and technology has advanced enough to make it possible, and instead use research to understand if the new feature will add value for our users. (We should also push back against collecting user data simply for sake of having it.) We'll cover responsible research and how to navigate mixed priorities from stakeholders in Chapter 5.

## CONNECTED WITHOUT CONSENT

The ability to track people's location and covertly surveil them is enabled in many unexpected apps and services. In her conference talk "Next Lvl Stalkerware," Cecilie Wian, a technologist in Norway, explained how she uncovered one such example after a visit to the grocery store to purchase tea for her office. Later that night, her partner asked, "Where's that tea you bought today?" while rummaging through the kitchen (http://bkaprt.com/dfs37/03-14, video).

Much to Wian's surprise, her partner had seen the purchase through an app associated with the grocery store. Wian had never registered an account with the app, and she and her partner have separate debit cards—but the app connected her purchases to their shared bank account, assuming that because they shared the account, they'd consented to sharing additional information about every transaction. He was able to see everything she had purchased, a timestamp of when the purchases were made, and the location of the store she visited.

Her partner hadn't set out to monitor her purchases or the time and location of her shopping trips. He had registered the app on his own phone under his own name, and the information about his partner was provided to him without him having to do anything except share a bank account with her. The app assumed her consent without actually receiving it.

This level of information access can easily enable stalking, financial abuse, elder abuse, and child abuse. Lists of purchases may not seem at first like a deep invasion of privacy, but consider that alcohol, tobacco, magazines, menstrual products, pregnancy tests, and sometimes the morning-after pill are all available in Norwegian grocery stores (as well as those in many other countries). Those monitoring their significant other's purchases might learn their partner suspects they're pregnant or is terminating a pregnancy—either situation representing a loss of control for abusers, which often prompts them to regain control through violence. That said, abusers will use any information they can find against their victims, no matter how innocuous, to demand financial control or reinforce authority.

The ease of this surveillance and stalking is especially troubling: vulnerable groups don't even have to be users of the app and have no recourse if they're being targeted. Wian only learned that her information had been shared in the app because her partner told her instead of keeping it secret; others may not be so lucky. Abusers could watch purchases for clues that a partner is making an escape plan and use the timestamp data to figure out if a victim made another stop between checking out from the store and arriving home. And it's easy to imagine how an abuser could weaponize the grocery store location and time their ex-partner was shopping to follow them to their new home, derailing the work of a survivor to leave an abuser and prevent further stalking and contact.

Wian took the admirable approach of working with the company to fix the problem in good faith, but after first promising to fix the issue, the company decided to leave the app as it was. Wian didn't give up—she contacted a tech journalist at Norway's largest news site (http://bkaprt.com/dfs37/03-15, in Norwegian). After the story broke, the company followed through with removing the feature that facilitated secret surveillance.

**Don't assume consent to connect**

Because Wian had consented to a joint bank account with her partner, the grocery store assumed her consent to participate in the app account as well. A better design would have alerted her that her purchase information and store location would be visible to her partner; a safer design wouldn't have allowed this scenario in the first place. Her partner's use of the app should have, at most, triggered an invitation to her to join his account on the app—not automatically shared a nonuser's information.

Consenting to a joint account with another person does not mean consenting to other joint accounts with that person. Products with the potential to link to other services where a joint account has been established must get consent from both parties rather than assuming that previous consent to one activity equals future consent to another.

## USER EXPERIENCE AND USER SAFETY TRADE-OFFS

A few years ago, I was staffed on a project for a large professional membership organization. My team was redesigning the flow for membership renewal, and our stakeholders wanted to let users into the flow using only their name and birthday as opposed to logging in. This would speed up the process for users renewing their membership—but my team lead pointed out that the flow included showing the user's address, which could put some of those users in danger. Birthdates aren't typically closely guarded information, and an abuser could easily find a survivor's new address through such a design. The client agreed, and we built a flow that prompted users to log in to renew their membership, protecting the sensitive information.

Unfortunately, many voter registration websites don't err on the side of safety, which puts survivors at odds with safe civic participation. Marleigh Farlow, an activist and survivor I spoke with shortly before the 2020 presidential election, described her struggles to keep her address private when registering to vote. Some voter registration systems, including the one in her home state, require only someone's name and birthday to reveal their address and its associated polling location.

For people who have no reason to worry about their address being so easily available, this makes for a good experience. But as we now know, there are millions of people stalked each year in the US who have to consider the safety implications of their address being available to anyone who knows their name and birthday. While some states have programs that allow residents to register and keep their address hidden, these programs often have high barriers to participation, such as providing a current restraining order (which not every stalking victim has or is able to obtain). Without a better solution, too many people with privacy concerns are forced into making a difficult decision between safety and civic participation.

## Enforce strict identify verification measures

No system should give private information, especially an address, to anyone who knows very basic information about someone.

A handful of states require a driver's license or state ID number, or the last four digits of the user's social security number, or both, in order to register to vote and view registration information. The addition of this private information makes the address on the other side of the voter registration system much harder for others to access.

## You will need some information about yourself to register

Please have the following information and materials to complete registration:

- Full Name
- Email
- Birthdate
- Social Security Number (SSN) or Individual Tax Identification Number (ITIN)
- Tax filing status
- Current address

Do you have this information available?

YES >

NO

**FIG 3.8:** Registering with the IRS website requires information less likely to be known by others, such as the user's social security number, which makes for a safer design than only requiring a name and birthday.

Farlow pointed to the IRS website as a good example of requiring more detailed personal information so a user can gain access (**FIG 3.8**). The IRS requires a user's name, birthday, social security number, and tax filing status to register, and the user's identity is then verified through a financial account, such as a credit card or student loan.

This increased barrier means it's more work for the user to create their account and access their tax information, but also makes it more difficult for others to view their personal information, which is a much safer experience. While we don't all need to be as thorough as the IRS (and should consider that not everyone has access to things like bank accounts), we should err on the side of user safety and require more than very basic identity information, which many abusers would likely know or be able to find, before revealing a user's location data.

## CONSIDER STALKING IN EVERY SCENARIO

Tech-enabled stalking shows up in some seriously sneaky ways. While methods like the Location Sharing feature on Google Maps are well known and easy to understand, there are a plethora of more insidious approaches to stalking that require technologists to be vigilant about identifying how our products and services might aid an unwanted pursuer. Next we'll look at a related topic that can be just as dangerous to those planning an escape from an abuser or trying to stay hidden from a stalker: covert surveillance.

# 4

# SURVEILLANCE AND THE STRUGGLE FOR PRIVACY

JASON AND MIA GOT THEIR first home surveillance camera when they had a baby, which quickly became two cameras after baby number two came along, and then four as both kids became more mobile and began to play outside. Mia loves that she can monitor her kids while away on business trips and often checks in on them to settle their arguments or simply relieve a moment of personal anxiety about how they're doing.

But as the number of cameras increases, so does Mia's watchfulness. One day while she's out of town, she sees that Jason ordered pizza for dinner and sends him a text: "Aren't there fresh veggies in the fridge?" Another day, their older daughter brings three friends home with her, and as they settle in to watch TV together, Mia alerts Jason again: "She needs to be focusing on homework. Tell her she can see her friends at school."

Jason feels like she's remotely watching and critiquing everything that goes on in the house. He hates the feeling that even when he thinks he's alone, his wife might be watching him and judging his behavior.

One day, after taking his kids to the doctor, he gives them ice cream as a reward for their good behavior, but the oldest is hesitant to eat it, and keeps glancing nervously at the nearest camera. When Jason asks her what's wrong, she answers: "I don't want to get in trouble for eating too much ice cream. Mom's always watching."

Mia insists that what she's doing is simply good parenting and that if she stopped monitoring her family "things would just fall apart." But Jason worries about the impact on their kids. How can they learn to be independent if their mom is constantly watching and telling them what to do?

Jason's concerns aren't out of line. In this chapter, we'll look at some of the impacts that intensive monitoring can have on children, the frightening abuse realities of stalkerware, and the ways surveillance tech endangers everyday people. How might we begin making surveillance products safer to use—or do we need to use them at all?

## MODERN SURVEILLANCE: PERVASIVE AND INVASIVE

Modern technology has made surveillance—both open and covert, done by governments, institutions, and individuals—easier than ever before. The proliferation of home security cameras, now relatively cheap and easy to install, has transformed our society into one in which surveillance is just a part of life.

Abusive partners use products ostensibly meant to increase security to invade their victims' privacy. A survivor in Winnipeg, who had moved with her children away from her abusive ex-husband, called the police after noticing an unusual hole in an electrical outlet in her bedroom. Authorities found a Nest camera in the outlet, pointed right at her bed, and another in the wall of her living room—secretly installed by her ex-husband. "All this time that I've worked so hard for him to be away from us, he was right here in this very house," the survivor said. "My sense of safety, my sense of trust is all gone" (http://bkaprt.com/dfs37/04-01).

It's not just abusive partners who secretly surveil others through home cameras: the normalization of cameras seems to bring out the voyeur in nearly everyone. When a *Washington Post* journalist interviewed fifty owners of indoor and outdoor camera systems, most people admitted that they were doing much more than catching package thieves:

*[Most] replied that they were fine with intimate new levels of surveillance—as long as they were the ones who got to watch. They analyzed their neighbors. They monitored their kids and house guests. And they judged the performance of housekeepers, babysitters and other domestic workers, often without letting them know they were being recorded. (http://bkaprt. com/dfs37/04-02)*

Being connected to the internet, home cameras are vulnerable to hacking: the *Washington Post* article mentions multiple cases of data breaches that opened up people's homes to total strangers who took advantage of the holes in security. Even without a data breach, the risk can come from a much closer source. Security company ADT came under fire in early 2021 with news that one of their employees had added himself to the accounts of over two hundred customers, particularly women he found attractive, in order to spy on them while they undressed and had sex (http://bkaprt.com/dfs37/04-03).

Despite the well-documented use of surveillance tech in domestic abuse contexts, personal and mass surveillance tools have gained normalcy in our society, and it can be difficult for safety-minded technologists to resist building features that enable monitoring. We have a responsibility to stand up to surveillance becoming a fixed part of life. The examples in this chapter may be useful support for the difficult conversations we need to have about how surveilling-enabling features will be used for abuse.

# THE AMAZON INVASION

Amazon is leading the way with abuse-ready surveillance products. The company continues to release new products that have problematic privacy implications, as well as retrofitting and updating older products to increase the potential for surveillance. For example, a 2020 launch event announced that the Echo Show 10, a 10-inch screen with a camera and smart speaker, was updated to include a swivel monitor that follows the user's movement so it can always face them (http://bkaprt. com/dfs37/04-04).

For certain use cases, such as a user always being able to view a recipe while cooking, this design makes sense. But considering it can also be activated by someone remotely and used as a security camera that can move around to see the whole room, it's easy to see how a product like this would make abusive surveillance all the more effective.

The launch event also included information about a new drone camera that zooms around a home on a preplanned path. An Amazon official stated that privacy isn't an issue for their new home surveillance drone because it's noisy: "It's built to be loud so it's privacy you can hear" (http://bkaprt. com/dfs37/04-05). A third product rolled out at the launch came from Ring (which is owned by Amazon): the company hopes to soon add car cameras to its lineup of video doorbells and home security systems.

No matter where the camera, the risk of people secretly surveilling their family members is high. There's also the reality that the upcoming Ring Car Cam will record nonusers, or people who are recorded without consent simply by walking past the car, just as people are currently recorded walking past the homes where Ring's doorbell cameras are installed.

Amazon profits off their customers' fears and unbridled desires to monitor everyone in their lives, from spouses to nameless delivery drivers. And while reducing unknowns can help people feel more secure, the reality is that these products are released with few, if any, safeguards in place to prevent them from being used to nonconsensually monitor others. How might products like these be designed safely rather than in a manner that all but ensures users will transform them into tools of abuse?

## Make cameras and recording explicit

Ring's installation guide urges users to "Make sure your Ring device is visible, so guests will know they are being captured on video." It explains that packages include a sticker to affix near the camera to let people know the home is protected by a Ring device that captures both video and audio.

The recommendation to "make it clear you're protected by Ring" suggests that Ring camera designers do understand the potential abuse case of a user secretly surveilling people in their homes. But the solution they propose is to provide a single sticker and leave it up to the individual to place it near the device. The idea that an abuser would willingly let their victim know about their home surveillance system is laughable; even among nonabusers, interviews with Ring owners show that many people use their Rings to secretly watch people in their homes (http://bkaprt.com/dfs37/04-02). The stickers are probably going right into the trash.

There are multiple solutions to the problem of secret surveillance (apart from enforcing wiretapping laws, which we'll look at in a bit—and which most of these companies disregard). One is to make recording extremely explicit: cameras could verbally announce their presence or flash a light to make it clear that they're there. We could design cameras to only function if one of the provided stickers is visible within its point of view. In the case of the Echo Show, we might alert anyone in the room when it's been remotely activated by someone else, so that they know there's a possibility they're being watched. Companies who invest in dedicated teams to work in this space would likely uncover even more ideas to reduce the abuse cases that their surveillance tech currently empowers.

# A PROBLEMATIC APPROACH TO LAWS AND LAW ENFORCEMENT

Ring does little to help its users understand the laws around surveillance and wiretapping they may be violating by using the product. Audio surveillance laws vary from state to state, and although law enforcement has been keen to use video footage from private Ring cameras, legal experts agree that the audio of such recordings fall into untested legal territory.

For example, twelve states require that all parties in a conversation consent to audio recording, meaning that in those states, using Ring cameras to capture both footage and audio may well be illegal. New Hampshire is one such state, and wiretapping laws made recording others without their permission illegal in 1969. But this hasn't stopped lawyers from attempting to use the audio footage of recorded crimes, such as in the 2020 case of a man shooting his brother on a driveway while a neighbor's Ring camera recorded (http://bkaprt.com/dfs37/04-06).

Cases like this will continue to test the legal boundaries of devices like Ring cameras, but until the laws are clarified, legal experts agree that in states like New Hampshire, people should avoid violating wiretapping laws by turning off audio recording on devices such as home Ring cameras.

However, instead of providing users with information about relevant laws in their state, Ring's installation guide simply says to "Respect your neighbors and your local laws" and advises users to avoid recording "public spaces and neighboring properties if necessary." Never mind that most buyers will reasonably assume that if this product is on the market, using it as the advertising suggests is within their legal rights. Ring's social media site, called Neighbors, further encourages users to record and share everything they can—bringing formerly private spaces (and the strangers passing through them) into the totally public view of the internet (http://bkaprt.com/dfs37/04-07).

When it comes to supporting law enforcement's desire to use Ring footage in their investigations, Ring has shown itself to be just as casual about users' rights as it is about helping them obey wiretapping laws. Amazon has partnered with police departments to help them request footage from Ring cameras without warrants or other judicial oversight. In exchange, cities are assisting with marketing efforts by encouraging residents to buy the cameras, sometimes using taxpayer dollars to subsidize the purchase (http://bkaprt.com/dfs37/04-08). Complicating the issue are the good intentions of city council members who believe the devices could actually help prevent crime and make people safer. One of these initiatives, in San Antonio, specifically aims to help survivors of domestic violence by giving them free Ring devices (http://bkaprt.com/dfs37/04-09). Critics of these programs have been quick to point out the myriad problems that could emerge by setting up, effectively, a citywide surveillance system under the control of a private corporation.

## Give legal information to users

A quick online search revealed that in states like Illinois, where I live, people have a right to privacy within their own homes—even from their spouses (http://bkaprt.com/dfs37/04-10). That means that it's typically illegal to secretly surveil an adult family member in their own home. And while this doesn't apply to secretly recording other people in your home, such as babysitters or dog walkers, it is illegal to record audio without permission in certain states. This means that to legally record someone like a nanny or house cleaner in my home without their knowledge using a Ring, I'd have to disable its audio recording feature.

This is the type of specific information that Ring should include within its setup documentation, rather than a vague suggestion to follow your local laws. The responsibility should fall on the company to inform users about laws they must observe when using their product. A truly ethical installation guide might also include a reminder that secretly recording people in your home can be a breach of trust, and that Ring use can also impact mental health; some users feel an increase in anxiety because of the hypervigilance the Ring app supports (http://bkaprt.com/dfs37/04-11).

## PROBLEMS WITH PASSWORDS

The speediest, most friction-free experience for most products is to design them so people can begin using them right out of the box; no password resets or identity verification needed. But when it comes to recording devices that live inside people's homes, the safety implications make this far from a reasonable trade-off. A streamlined user experience simply isn't worth it when the impact of foregoing essential security best practices is real and severe safety issues.

A 2019 *Guardian* article detailed multiple reports describing people hacking into Ring cameras, often quite easily, because owners were never prompted to change the default password. Some hackers spoke directly to children in the house in unnerving exchanges; another demanded a $350,000 bitcoin ransom from a couple. One victim later sued the company for allowing the hacking to occur, specifically calling out that the devices did not require users to create complicated passwords or use two-factor authentication to verify their identities (http:// bkaprt.com/dfs37/04-12).

In addition to allowing hackers access, poor security practices for Ring devices meant that even changing the password to remove an unwanted user was useless because Ring failed to log out all users after someone had taken the action of changing their password. The situation was doubly problematic because after changing your password, it's usually a safe assumption that you've given unwelcome users the boot; it's a standard security practice for hacking victims and domestic violence survivors alike. But for a long time this wasn't the case with Ring cameras, and people had no idea that it hadn't worked. It didn't matter how much time had passed; the app never asked other users to sign in again after a password change.

As reported by Reed Albergotti for The Information, this was a major problem for Ring user Jesus Echezarreta, whose ex-boyfriend was able to continue to watch him through his Ring camera even after Echezarreta changed the password on two separate occasions. His ex also downloaded multiple videos from Echezarreta's doorbell and would sometimes use the app to make the doorbell ring in the middle of the night, waking

Echezarreta up and causing him to go to his front door, only to find no one there.

After users began to contact Ring about the security issue, the company updated the app to log out all users after a password change, but a subsequent test showed logging out all users took several hours. CEO Jamie Siminoff acknowledged that the app didn't log users out immediately, saying that to follow this security best practice would slow down the app too much. This is a situation where safety needs to be prioritized over speed (http://bkaprt.com/dfs37/04-13).

## Follow basic security best practices

These stories of how poor security practices put users in danger, both from anonymous hackers and from known individuals, illustrate the need to follow security best practices—and show that these standards aren't always a given. And while security might seem outside the realm of designers, it's not. More often than not, it falls to a designer to create user flows that include choosing a unique, complex password when setting up the account, and to developers to build the capacity to verify the user's identity with something like two-factor authentication.

Next time you're working on the design or build for an account access interface, ask if it protects users by:

- using two-factor authentication or another method of verifying the user's identity,
- guiding the user through changing the default password the first time they use the product, and then instructing users on how to change passwords,
- requiring a strong password (a mix of numbers, letters, and symbols, with both uppercase and lowercase letters), and
- logging out all users when the password is changed.

See the Resources section for the Open Web Application Security Project's (OWASP) top ten web app security risks. This resource is a great jumping-off point for technologists to learn more about security.

We don't need to be security experts to build these processes into our wireframes, project plans, and codebases. Especially at companies with small or nonexistent security teams, we must all embrace the basic best practices as we develop products.

## STALKERWARE

Stalkerware (also known as "spyware" and sometimes "spouserware") is different from the other examples in this chapter, as it isn't a product that was built for something legitimate and then becomes weaponized for abuse: the intention of the product is malicious. By definition, stalkerware is designed and built to secretly monitor and track others without their consent.

The Coalition Against Stalkerware, which unites advocacy groups, survivors, technologists, and security firms to combat technology-facilitated stalking and abuse, defines stalkerware as software that is:

> *made available directly to individuals, that enables a remote user to monitor the activities on another user's device without that user's consent and without explicit, persistent notification to that user in a manner that may facilitate intimate partner surveillance, harassment, abuse, stalking, and/or violence. (http://bkaprt.com/dfs37/04-14)*

Most of these products don't include any UI elements that could alert the user that they're being monitored, with some even boasting that the monitoring is completely hidden. This means there are almost no safeguards in place to stop adults using stalkerware on the devices of nonconsenting adults.

In 2018, the *New York Times* identified over two hundred apps and services that cater to would-be stalkers, with features ranging from location tracking to recovering deleted text messages from a victim's phone. Many of these products focus their marketing on "keeping children safe online" while actually offering features, as well as user support, suited to secretly monitoring a significant other (http://bkaprt.com/dfs37/04-15).

**FIG 4.1:** Stalkerware manufacturers intentionally appeal to abusers' fear of losing control over their victims. (Screenshot taken August 29, 2020, from TheTruthSpy)

Spyware product TheTruthSpy, for example, has a plethora of articles catering to users who want to secretly monitor a significant other's device, with imagery that suggests the victim is doing something secretive and wrong that needs to be uncovered (which, to be clear, would not justify secret monitoring even if it were the case). The reality is, abusers are eager to have power and control over every aspect of their victim's life, and monitoring their devices is an effective way to achieve that goal (**FIG 4.1**).

One example of just how dangerous these products can be involves a product called MobiStealth, which is linked to two separate domestic violence murders. In 2012, a Florida man murdered his wife after secretly monitoring the calls, texts, and emails on her mobile phone, which he claimed gave him proof she was cheating on him (http://bkaprt.com/dfs37/04-16). And in

2011, an Australian man used the app to secretly read his fiancée's text messages. When he read that she was making plans to escape the abusive relationship, he threw her off the balcony of their fifteenth-floor apartment, killing her (http://bkaprt.com/dfs37/04-17). Not only do stalkerware apps like MobiStealth disregard people's right to privacy (and we'll explore the way these companies skirt laws next), but they also make crucial elements to surviving domestic violence, such as secretly planning an escape from the relationship, difficult or impossible.

## Legal gray areas

There are plenty of current laws that prohibit stalking, but there's little on the books to prevent location tracking—meaning that spyware products exist in a legal gray area. It's also legal for people to install location-tracking software on their own phones, giving abusers legal cover if they purchased the phone that their victim uses.

Similar to Ring, stalkerware companies typically include fine print telling their users that it's their responsibility to know and follow local, state, and federal laws, absolving themselves of any responsibility for how their users choose to use (and misuse) their product. Covered legally by that fine print, many companies openly market themselves to abusers and wash their hands of the knowledge that their products are being used for illegal, abusive, and even deadly ends. The continued legality of designing, selling, and using stalkerware is a clear indicator that the rights of abusers have been prioritized over vulnerable users' rights to privacy and safety.

Law enforcement could successfully shut down the entire stalkerware market if they prioritized doing so, and there are a few signs of some progress in this area. In 2014, the Justice Department arrested and indicted the CEO of a company that sold a stalkerware product called StealthGenie, which focused on the "spousal cheat" market (http://bkaprt.com/dfs37/04-18). And in 2016, after a Texas man secretly installed spyware on his wife's computer, police charged him with unlawful interception of electronic information (http://bkaprt.com/dfs37/04-19).

While these events are encouraging, they have not led to more prosecutions or stalkerware products leaving the market. Legislative action is also at a standstill: in 2005, the House of Representatives passed the Internet Spyware Prevention Act but it never moved on to become a law (http://bkaprt.com/dfs37/04-20).

The fact that these products are not themselves illegal, despite being created to enable illegal activities, is strange to me. Many products used for crimes, such as cars and guns, are legal because they have lawful use cases, and are also regulated by the government (though guns need far more regulation to prevent them being used criminally). Unlike those products, spyware has no legitimate use case or regulation. It is urgent that lawmakers update antistalking laws to prohibit these sorts of products and that stalkerware companies are held accountable for their role in unlawful surveillance.

## What about the children?

Many stalkerware companies operate under the guise of "protecting children online," marketing their products to parents worried about their children's internet activity. Kids are indeed vulnerable to harm from bullies and bad actors across digital platforms, from social media to internet forums to simple text messages. Stalkerware companies argue that the answer to this risk is to secretly monitor your child's digital activities.

The marketing behind these products typically implies that secretly monitoring a child's device is the only way to find out what's really going on with them (**FIG 4.2**). Stalkerware apps stand to profit by convincing parents that their kids can't be trusted—a premise that often damages those relationships even further.

When parents secretly monitor their children's online activity, or demand account passwords so they can look at their children's social media messages, it can set a dangerous precedent about what constitutes normal, healthy behavior within a loving relationship. Danah Boyd, the founder of Data & Society, described how she was disturbed when her fieldwork with teenagers revealed that the problematic privacy norms estab-

**Jennifer**
AZ, USA

Something weird was happening to my daughter. She was always in a bad mood and wouldn't come out of her room. Every time she got a message, she looked like she was about to cry. I tried talking to her, but she refused to come clean. That's when I found mSpy™. I looked through her chats, and it turned out that she was bullied by her classmates! They kept sending offensive jokes and made awful photoshopped pictures of her. I went to the principal with the screenshots, and the school helped me to handle the situation.

**Thomas**
Bonn, Germany

I would have never in my life thought that my son would get into online gambling. He wasn't the type of person to mess with such things. At least I thought he wasn't. Then I found out that all of my secret savings were gone. I thought we were robbed, but then I noticed that my son was unusually anxious and fidgety. Of course, he would deny anything. I searched for a way to check his messages without touching his phone and found mSpy™. Thank God we managed to stop this whole deal before it was too late.

**Clara**
Lyon, France

I've heard a lot about the victims of online predators but never thought my daughter would become one of them. mSpy™ helped me to bust a man who sent my 14-year-old daughter inappropriate texts and disgusting photos. I could not believe my eyes! He was trying to lure her into meeting him and running away together. I don't want to even imagine what would have happened if we hadn't found out about it on time.

**FIG 4.2:** Who can you trust: your lying teenager, or this spyware app? Testimonials for mSpy portray concern for kids' well-being, but don't mention the damage that intensive, nonconsensual monitoring can do to a child's sense of trust.

lished by their parents were often recreated in their relationships with their peers.

Boyd found that teenagers would often share social media passwords with their significant others as a demonstration of trust, using the same justifications that their parents used with them. "They learned this from watching us and from the language we used when we explained why we demanded to have their passwords." Boyd also warned that when parents monitor their children, often "the sharing of information isn't a mutual sign of trust and respect but a process of surveillance" (http://bkaprt.com/dfs37/04-21).

It's also critical to note that surveillance typically doesn't remain secret or even effective. The average teen is more tech-savvy than their parents, especially when it comes to new technology (http://bkaprt.com/dfs37/04-22). And once they realize they're being monitored, they're often able to find ways to evade the surveillance, using everything from in-app settings that turn off location settings when the battery is low to simply leaving their phone at a friend's house when sneaking out, ironically putting the child in a more dangerous situation than if their parent had never installed the surveillance software in the first place (**FIG 4.3**).

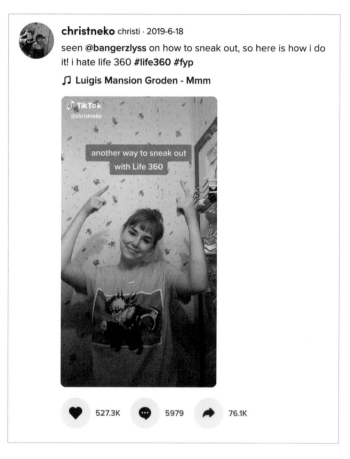

FIG 4.3: TikTok user christneko is one of many teens helping her peers evade parental surveillance through the popular Life360 app (http://bkaprt.com/dfs37/04-23).

Privacy, both online and off, is important to teenagers for a multitude of reasons, but it's paramount for those who need to explore their gender and sexual identities in a way that won't tip off homophobic parents. A 2015 article published in the *Guardian* detailed the story of a young man who had his homosexuality outed to his unsupportive parents through stalkerware (http://bkaprt.com/dfs37/04-24). In a different article, a mother describes how her daughter's friend was outed because the friend had sent snapchat messages about her sexuality to a third friend, whose mother consistently read her communications (http://bkaprt.com/dfs37/04-25).

According to a study by the National Gay and Lesbian Task Force Policy Institute and the National Coalition for the Homeless, LGBTQ+ youth experience homelessness at a disproportionate rate. One study found that 50 percent of gay teens received a negative reaction from their parents when they came out, with 26 percent being kicked out of their homes. Considering this reality, preventing LGBTQ+ teens from being secretly monitored, by their own parents or their friends' parents, is especially important.

Attorney Christina Nguyen proposed a quality solution for ensuring consent, at least in Washington state, in a 2016 paper that argued for expanding legislation to ensure that children know they are being monitored and consent to it (http://bkaprt. com/dfs37/04-26). The most secure way to get that consent would be for the distributor of the monitoring software to act as witness to the process. Just as with any other legal or financial witnessing, consent would need to be obtained in person, or else it would be too easy to falsify. Parents would then only be allowed to install and use the monitoring software after obtaining their child's consent.

## Don't let stalkers hide behind software

Secretly surveilling another person without their consent is unethical, exists in a legal gray area, and is often, if not always, used for nefarious, abusive, or dangerous purposes. True, it is not illegal to install tracking software on a phone you own; but there's no reason that this tracking software should be able to stay completely hidden from the person using the phone. All monitoring software, even products meant to monitor children, should have a UI element that makes it clear that surveillance is taking place. Since this means the software is no longer secret, it is no longer technically stalkerware.

**Identify stalkerware as a virus**

While we wait for marketing and legislation to make stalkerware a thing of the past, Eva Galperin, director of cyber security for the digital civil liberties group Electronic Frontier Foundation, has been working with antivirus companies to include the detection of stalkerware in their products (http://bkaprt. com/dfs37/04-27). Most antivirus software can detect stalkerware on a user's machine, but do not classify it as malware or a virus, allowing it to remain on the device unreported. Antivirus company Kapersky has committed to flagging stalkerware in its detection services, and in August 2020, the company announced spyware defense for PC users. Hopefully more antivirus companies will follow Kapersky's lead.

## RESIST SURVEILLANCE

The recent surge of surveillance tech and its ability to surveil our lives in increasingly intimate ways has opened the doors for new forms of abuse and control. Technologists must resist building unethical surveillance products, such as stalkerware, and ensure that safeguards are built into the rest.

So far, this book has covered a range of ways that technology is weaponized for harm. Between unethical surveillance, the problems with location data, and the struggle to ensure proper control between users, there are a lot of things to consider when it comes to designing for safety. The next chapter will explain the nuts and bolts of designing for safety, including how to identify these problems before they occur, and tips for convincing your stakeholders that this work is worth spending time on.

# 5 INTEGRATING SAFETY INTO YOUR PRACTICE

ANTIRACIST ECONOMIST KIM CRAYTON says that "intention without strategy is chaos." We've discussed how our biases, assumptions, and inattention toward marginalized and vulnerable groups lead to dangerous and unethical tech—but what, *specifically*, do we need to do to fix it? The intention to make our tech safer is not enough; we need a strategy.

This chapter will equip you with that plan of action. It covers how to integrate safety principles into your design work in order to create tech that's safe, how to convince your stakeholders that this work is necessary, and how to respond to the critique that what we *actually* need is more diversity. (Spoiler: we do, but diversity alone is not the antidote to fixing unethical, unsafe tech.)

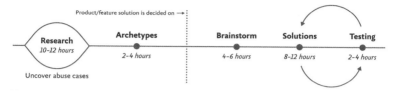

Product/feature solution is decided on →

Research
10-12 hours

Uncover abuse cases

Archetypes
2-4 hours

Brainstorm
4-6 hours

Solutions
8-12 hours

Testing
2-4 hours

Total time: 24-32 hours (3-4 days)

FIG 5.1: Each aspect of the Process for Inclusive Safety can be incorporated into your design process where it makes the most sense for you. The times given are estimates to help you incorporate the stages into your design plan.

---

## THE PROCESS FOR INCLUSIVE SAFETY

When you are designing for safety, your goals are to:

- identify ways your product can be used for abuse,
- design ways to prevent the abuse, and
- provide support for vulnerable users to reclaim power and control.

The Process for Inclusive Safety is a tool to help you reach those goals (FIG 5.1). It's a methodology I created in 2018 to capture the various techniques I was using when designing products with safety in mind. Whether you are creating an entirely new product or adding to an existing feature, the Process can help you make your product safe and inclusive. The Process includes five general areas of action:

- Conducting research
- Creating archetypes
- Brainstorming problems
- Designing solutions
- Testing for safety

The Process is meant to be flexible—it won't make sense for teams to implement every step in some situations. Use the parts that are relevant to your unique work and context; this is meant to be something you can insert into your existing design practice. And once you use it, if you have an idea for making it better or simply want to provide context of how it helped your team, please get in touch with me. It's a living document that I hope will continue to be a useful and realistic tool that technologists can use in their day-to-day work.

If you're working on a product specifically for a vulnerable group or survivors of some form of trauma, such as an app for survivors of domestic violence, sexual assault, or drug addiction, be sure to read Chapter 7, which covers that situation explicitly and should be handled a bit differently. The guidelines here are for prioritizing safety when designing a more general product that will have a wide user base (which, we already know from statistics, will include certain groups that should be protected from harm). Chapter 7 is focused on products that are *specifically for* vulnerable groups and people who have experienced trauma.

## Step 1: Conduct research

Design research should include a broad analysis of how your tech might be weaponized for abuse as well as specific insights into the experiences of survivors and perpetrators of that type of abuse. At this stage, you and your team will investigate issues of interpersonal harm and abuse, and explore any other safety, security, or inclusivity issues that might be a concern for your product or service, like data security, racist algorithms, and harassment.

### Broad research

Your project should begin with broad, general research into similar products and issues around safety and ethical concerns that have already been reported. For example, a team building a smart home device would do well to understand the multitude of ways that existing smart home devices have been used as tools of abuse. If your product will involve AI, seek to understand the potentials for racism and other issues that have been reported in existing AI products. Nearly all types of technology have some kind of potential or actual harm that's been reported on in the news or written about by academics. Google Scholar is a useful tool for finding these studies (http:// bkaprt.com/dfs37/05-01).

## Specific research: Survivors

When possible and appropriate, include direct research (surveys and interviews) with people who are experts in the forms of harm you have uncovered. Ideally, you'll want to interview advocates working in the space of your research first so that you have a more solid understanding of the topic and are better equipped to not retraumatize survivors. If you've uncovered possible domestic violence issues, for example, the experts you'll want to speak with are survivors themselves, as well as workers at domestic violence hotlines, shelters, other related nonprofits, and lawyers.

Especially when interviewing survivors of any kind of trauma, it is important to pay people for their knowledge and lived experiences. Don't ask survivors to share their trauma for free, as this is exploitative. While some survivors may not want to be paid, you should always make the offer in the initial ask. An alternative to payment is to donate to an organization working against the type of violence that the interviewee experienced. We'll talk more about how to appropriately interview survivors in Chapter 6.

## Specific research: Abusers

It's unlikely that teams aiming to design for safety will be able to interview self-proclaimed abusers or people who have broken laws around things like hacking. Don't make this a goal; rather, try to get at this angle in your general research. Aim to understand how abusers or bad actors weaponize technology to use against others, how they cover their tracks, and how they explain or rationalize the abuse.

## Harry Oleson

### Goals

**Stalk his ex-girlfriend Sarah through her fitness products**

Harry knows the general area Sarah moved to after their breakup, even if he hasn't been able to figure out her new address. He knows that she's an avid runner, and when the two were together, they followed each other on their various fitness apps and products. But now, Sarah has unfollowed him and set all of her accounts to private. Harry is constantly on the look out for some kind of loophole, regularly checking her profiles and exploring new features for any opportunity to further pinpoint her location.

Photo attribute: Tom Wheatley, Unsplash

**FIG 5.2:** Harry Oleson, an abuser archetype for a fitness product, is looking for ways to stalk his ex-girlfriend through the fitness apps she uses.

## Step 2: Create archetypes

Once you've finished conducting your research, use your insights to create abuser and survivor archetypes. Archetypes are not personas, as they're not based on real people that you interviewed and surveyed. Instead, they're based on your research into likely safety issues, much like when we design for accessibility: we don't need to have found a group of blind or low-vision users in our interview pool to create a design that's inclusive of them. Instead, we base those designs on existing research into what this group needs. Personas typically represent real users and include many details, while archetypes are broader and can be more generalized.

The abuser archetype is someone who will look at the product as a tool to perform harm (**FIG 5.2**). They may be trying to harm someone they don't know through surveillance or anon-

# Lisa Zwaan

## Goals

**Confirm that her husband Ben is using their home's IoT devices to monitor her activity, harass, terrify, and gaslight her.**

Lisa suspects that her husband is using IoT devices to scare her, such as turning out the lights when she's home alone at night, but he's so insistent that it's not him, and that she's simply using the products wrong, that she has a lingering doubt about whether or not she can trust her instincts. She wishes she could prove without a doubt that Ben's the one doing these things.

**Understand how to "record" or "prove" that her husband is abusing her through IoT devices.**

Lisa is in the process of safety planning and plotting her escape. She also plans to file a police report, and has been collecting evidence of his abuse, such as photos of bruises, but isn't sure how she can collect evidence of the abuse that's happening via all the home IoT devices.

Photo attribute: #WOCinTech Chat

**FIG 5.3:** The survivor archetype Lisa Zwaan suspects her husband is weaponizing their home's IoT devices against her, but in the face of his insistence that she simply doesn't understand how to use the products, she's unsure. She needs some kind of proof of the abuse.

ymous harassment, or they may be trying to control, monitor, abuse, or torment someone they know personally.

The survivor archetype is someone who is being abused with the product. There are various situations to consider in terms of the archetype's understanding of the abuse and how to put an end to it: Do they need proof of abuse they already suspect is happening, or are they unaware they've been targeted in the first place and need to be alerted (**FIG 5.3**)?

You may want to make multiple survivor archetypes to capture a range of different experiences. They may know that the abuse is happening but not be able to stop it, like when an abuser locks them out of IoT devices; or they know it's happening but don't know how, such as when a stalker keeps figuring out their location (**FIG 5.4**). Include as many of these

# Eric Mitchell

## Goals

**Understand how his ex-boyfriend is stalking him.**

Eric is being stalked by his ex-boyfriend Rob, and he can't figure out how Rob's doing it. His mission to figure out how Rob is finding his location has made him realize how little information his various apps and accounts give him when there's another user in the picture.

**Once he knows how Rob is stalking him, Eric needs to make it stop and ensure it can't happen again.**

Eric's worried that once he does figure it out, and removes Rob from the account or service that he was using to stalk him, that Rob will somehow easily be able to re-add himself or take the same action again and continue stalking him. He feels like he's going to have constantly keep watch on his apps and accounts to make sure Eric hasn't come back.

**FIG 5.4:** The survivor archetype Eric Mitchell knows he's being stalked by his ex-boyfriend Rob but can't figure out how Rob is learning his location information.

scenarios as you need to in your survivor archetype. You'll use these later on when you design solutions to help your survivor archetypes achieve their goals of preventing and ending abuse.

It may be useful for you to create persona-like artifacts for your archetypes, such as the three examples shown. Instead of focusing on the demographic information we often see in personas, focus on their goals. The goals of the abuser will be to carry out the specific abuse you've identified, while the goals of the survivor will be to prevent abuse, understand that abuse is happening, make ongoing abuse stop, or regain control over the technology that's being used for abuse. Later, you'll brainstorm how to prevent the abuser's goals and assist the survivor's goals.

And while the "abuser/survivor" model fits most cases, it doesn't fit all, so modify it as you need to. For example, if you uncovered an issue with security, such as the ability for someone to hack into a home camera system and talk to children, the malicious hacker would get the abuser archetype and the child's parents would get survivor archetype.

## Step 3: Brainstorm problems

After creating archetypes, brainstorm novel abuse cases and safety issues. "Novel" means things not found in your research; you're trying to identify completely *new* safety issues that are unique to your product or service. The goal with this step is to exhaust every effort of identifying harms your product could cause. You aren't worrying about how to prevent the harm yet—that comes in the next step.

How could your product be used for any kind of abuse, outside of what you've already identified in your research? I recommend setting aside at least a few hours with your team for this process.

If you're looking for somewhere to start, try doing a Black Mirror brainstorm. This exercise is based on the show *Black Mirror*, which features stories about the dark possibilities of technology. Try to figure out how your product would be used in an episode of the show—the most wild, awful, out-of-control ways it could be used for harm. When I've led Black Mirror brainstorms, participants usually end up having a good deal of fun (which I think is great—it's okay to have fun when designing for safety!). I recommend time-boxing a Black Mirror brainstorm to half an hour, and then dialing it back and using the rest of the time thinking of more realistic forms of harm.

After you've identified as many opportunities for abuse as possible, you may still not feel confident that you've uncovered every potential form of harm. A healthy amount of anxiety is normal when you're doing this kind of work. It's common for teams designing for safety to worry, "Have we really identified every possible harm? What if we've missed something?" If you've spent at least four hours coming up with ways your product could be used for harm and have run out of ideas, go to the next step.

It's impossible to guarantee you've thought of everything; instead of aiming for 100 percent assurance, recognize that you've taken this time and have done the best you can, and commit to continuing to prioritize safety in the future. Once your product is released, your users may identify new issues that you missed; aim to receive that feedback graciously and course-correct quickly.

## Step 4: Design solutions

At this point, you should have a list of ways your product can be used for harm as well as survivor and abuser archetypes describing opposing user goals. The next step is to identify ways to design against the identified abuser's goals and to support the survivor's goals. This step is a good one to insert alongside existing parts of your design process where you're proposing solutions for the various problems your research uncovered.

Some questions to ask yourself to help prevent harm and support your archetypes include:

- Can you design your product in such a way that the identified harm cannot happen in the first place? If not, what roadblocks can you put up to prevent the harm from happening?
- How can you make the victim aware that abuse is happening through your product?
- How can you help the victim understand what they need to do to make the problem stop?
- Can you identify any types of user activity that would indicate some form of harm or abuse? Could your product help the user access support?

In some products, it's possible to proactively recognize that harm is happening. For example, a pregnancy app might be modified to allow the user to report that they were the victim of an assault, which could trigger an offer to receive resources for local and national organizations. This sort of proactiveness is not always possible, but it's worth taking a half hour to discuss if any type of user activity would indicate some form of harm or abuse, and how your product could assist the user in receiving help in a safe manner.

That said, use caution: you don't want to do anything that could put a user in harm's way if their devices are being monitored. If you do offer some kind of proactive help, always make it voluntary, and think through other safety issues, such as the need to keep the user in-app in case an abuser is checking their search history. We'll walk through a good example of this in the next chapter.

## Step 5: Test for safety

The final step is to test your prototypes from the point of view of your archetypes: the person who wants to weaponize the product for harm and the victim of the harm who needs to regain control over the technology. Just like any other kind of product testing, at this point you'll aim to rigorously test out your safety solutions so that you can identify gaps and correct them, validate that your designs will help keep your users safe, and feel more confident releasing your product into the world.

Ideally, safety testing happens along with usability testing. If you're at a company that doesn't do usability testing, you might be able to use safety testing to cleverly perform both; a user who goes through your design attempting to weaponize the product against someone else can also be encouraged to point out interactions or other elements of the design that don't make sense to them.

You'll want to conduct safety testing on either your final prototype or the actual product if it's already been released. There's nothing wrong with testing an existing product that wasn't designed with safety goals in mind from the onset—"retrofitting" it for safety is a good thing to do.

Remember that testing for safety involves testing from the perspective of both an abuser and a survivor, though it may not make sense for you to do both. Alternatively, if you made multiple survivor archetypes to capture multiple scenarios, you'll want to test from the perspective of each one.

As with other sorts of usability testing, you as the designer are most likely too close to the product and its design by this point to be a valuable tester; you know the product too well. Instead of doing it yourself, set up testing as you would with other usability testing: find someone who is not familiar with the product and its design, set the scene, give them a task, encourage them to think out loud, and observe how they attempt to complete it.

## Abuser testing

The goal of this testing is to understand how easy it is for someone to weaponize your product for harm. Unlike with usability testing, you *want* to make it impossible, or at least difficult, for them to achieve their goal. Reference the goals in the abuser archetype you created earlier, and use your product in an attempt to achieve them.

For example, for a fitness app with GPS-enabled location features, we can imagine that the abuser archetype would have the goal of figuring out where his ex-girlfriend now lives. With this goal in mind, you'd try everything possible to figure out the location of another user who has their privacy settings enabled. You might try to see her running routes, view any available information on her profile, view anything available about her location (which she has set to private), and investigate the profiles of any other users somehow connected with her account, such as her followers.

If by the end of this you've managed to uncover some of her location data, despite her having set her profile to private, you know now that your product enables stalking. Your next step is to go back to step 4 and figure out how to prevent this from happening. You may need to repeat the process of designing solutions and testing them more than once.

## Survivor testing

Survivor testing involves identifying how to give information and power to the survivor. It might not always make sense based on the product or context. Thwarting the attempt of an abuser archetype to stalk someone also satisfies the goal of the survivor archetype to not be stalked, so separate testing wouldn't be needed from the survivor's perspective.

However, there are cases where it makes sense. For example, for a smart thermostat, a survivor archetype's goals would be to understand who or what is making the temperature change when they aren't doing it themselves. You could test this by looking for the thermostat's history log and checking for usernames, actions, and times; if you couldn't find that information, you would have more work to do in step 4.

Another goal might be regaining control of the thermostat once the survivor realizes the abuser is remotely changing its settings. Your test would involve attempting to figure out how to do this: are there instructions that explain how to remove another user and change the password, and are they easy to find? This might again reveal that more work is needed to make it clear to the user how they can regain control of the device or account.

**Stress testing**

To make your product more inclusive and compassionate, consider adding stress testing. This concept comes from *Design for Real Life* by Eric Meyer and Sara Wachter-Boettcher. The authors pointed out that personas typically center people who are having a good day—but real users are often anxious, stressed out, having a bad day, or even experiencing tragedy. These are called "stress cases," and testing your products for users in stress-case situations can help you identify places where your design lacks compassion. *Design for Real Life* has more details about what it looks like to incorporate stress cases into your design as well as many other great tactics for compassionate design (http://bkaprt.com/dfs37/05-02).

## When prevention is impossible or imperfect

Sometimes a team goes through the process of identifying abuse cases and ways to prevent them but isn't able to come up with any effective solutions. In this scenario, the question to ask next is whether this product or feature is absolutely necessary when weighed against the abuse cases. If there's a chance that using the product for abuse could cause serious harm, you must engage in the difficult conversation of whether or not the product should exist.

In a perfect world, designers all over the globe would stand up against products used for abuse, halting their creation altogether. But we don't live in a perfect world, and a product has to be dangerous to the extreme to have technologists refuse to build it. Do the slight improvements in some people's lives—say, the ease of controlling their home's temperature and a modest reduction in energy costs—outweigh the fact that the technology will be used to gaslight, harass, and terrorize others?

Regardless of how you answer that question, it is unlikely that designers will be able to successfully prevent tech with abuse potential from entering the market—at least, not without significant changes to our institutions, which we'll discuss more in Chapter 8.

The practice of *design justice* says in these situations, we must be clear about which users we are prioritizing. If your team identifies that your product will be used for certain types of abuse, and that solutions to prevent the abuse are impossible or imperfect, that fact should be included in your artifacts and presentations. Make it clear to your stakeholders that the current design is prioritizing the convenience of abusers over the safety of their victims—and follow up with ideas for how power and control can be given to survivors of the abuse your product will enable.

## ENCOURAGING SUPPORT IN YOUR ORGANIZATION

The Process for Inclusive Safety will add some hours to your overall timeline. Most technologists are familiar with a fast-paced environment, pressure to ship, and stakeholders who have little patience (or budget) or anything they view as "extra" work.

Your approach to convincing stakeholders to pay for designing for safety will vary based on your company type (product, consultancy, etc.), internal culture, and individual stakeholders.

Ideally, you'd be able to simply say, "We need some time to make sure our product isn't able to be weaponized for harm against our users," and your stakeholders would say, "Of course." But as that's not everyone's reality, here are a few methods for convincing the people in charge to back your approach.

## Provide time specifics

Figure out which parts of the Process you'll need to incorporate, where they'll dovetail with your own process, and how much they'll add to your timeline. Look at the graphic of the Process for estimates of how many hours each step takes. Include the number of hours you'll need, as well as what you'll be doing during those hours, in the request you make to your stakeholders. It's easier to say yes to an exact number of hours than a nebulous estimate or no time frame at all.

## Provide design specifics

Do some initial thinking about how the product might be used for abuse, and include time in your overall project plan to expand upon that work and identify solutions. For example, if your team is designing a chat feature, you might indicate that people often use chat or message features for harassment— while stressing that further research could help your team identify methods for countering that potential.

Include some brief examples of the type of harm you intend to research, and tie them directly to improvements in your product. With a chat feature, you might explain that taking time to understand and prevent abusive chatting will result in not only better safety for your users but an overall improved user experience and fewer users turning to customer support services for help.

## Discuss safety in your scope of work

If you work somewhere that involves submitting a scope of work to a client, include safety design as a part of your overall design process. You might include language like:

*Many technology products can be used for harm, generating bad press and angry reviews. Our process aims to identify potentials for misuse and abuse and includes thoughtful design to reduce the likelihood of your product being weaponized for harm in a way that was never intended.*

This way, you've identified safety design as a standard part of your process rather than something you need to ask for extra time to do later.

This language is just a starting suggestion; you may want to get input from a legal advisor, project directors, or a sales team to make sure everyone's on board with the expectations you set in your contracts.

## Use statistics

Domestic violence is incredibly common to the human experience. As mentioned earlier, one in three women and one in four men in the US have experienced violence from their intimate partners (http://bkaprt.com/dfs37/00-01, PDF). I always have this statistic ready to go when talking about designing for safety.

This CDC statistic is the most relevant one for domestic violence; try to find similar statistics that pertain to your product and the potentials for abuse that you've identified. You'll want to memorize the most striking statistics (and where they came from) to bring present them in case a stakeholder argues that the abuse isn't prevalent enough to warrant spending time preventing it.

## Get uncomfortable

For the most part, people don't openly support things like domestic violence, stealing from elders, or surveilling people without their consent. I've found that as soon as one person brings up one of these issues, especially if they have a statistic to back them up, the rest of the group will often fall in line. However, being the first one to bring something like this up can feel awkward and difficult.

I've also found that being matter-of-fact works best. If your team is debating the necessity of informing someone their location is visible to others through a product's GPS, you could calmly say something like, "Well, considering one in six women get stalked, and just over half our user base is women, we should probably make sure we're doing our due diligence."

Doing this can be very uncomfortable. Practice saying it out loud. Memorize your relevant statistic (and its source, in case you've got an especially vocal naysayer in the room who questions the statistic's validity). Accept that it's going to feel pretty weird to bring it up. Whenever possible, talk to a supportive teammate (or multiple teammates) ahead of time about backing you up. This is an opportunity to practice allyship and vocally support keeping groups safe even if you don't belong to that group.

As a last-ditch effort, if your stakeholders aren't convinced that keeping people safe matters, you might bring up the potential for a public relations nightmare or even a lawsuit when a user is severely harmed by the product (which, as we've talked about before, *will* happen eventually when safety isn't considered and prioritized).

## SUPPORTING DIVERSE TEAMS

When a racist, sexist, or other harmful product gets a lot of press, critics often point at the abysmally low number of employees at the company who belong to the impacted group (and it's always abysmally low). Many of the overall issues of inequality in tech are framed as a diversity issue: if we just had teams with more women, more Black people, more Indigenous people, more queer people, more disabled people—if we simply had more people in tech from historically and currently excluded groups—then these issues would sort themselves out.

Take, for example, Google Photos coming under fire in 2015 when the service's algorithm automatically tagged photos of Black people with the term "gorillas." Many media reports framed the racist tagging as purely a diversity issue, blaming the low number of Black employees at Google as well as the low number of photos of Black people used to train the algorithm (http://bkaprt.com/dfs37/05-03).

These are fair conclusions, but we need to ask ourselves if simply adding in people from marginalized groups implies that individuals alone can fix broken institutions. Did the few Black employees already present at Google feel safe enough to raise their concerns about the lack of Black photos being used to train the algorithm? If they did bring up their unease, were they ignored or even punished for doing so? Was the person with ultimate decision-making power more or less likely to take these concerns seriously based on their own identities and life experiences?

## Diversity must be paired with equity and inclusion

While hiring more Black employees at Google is a good idea for many reasons, it can't be relied on as a quick fix to address problematic tech unless the company also makes sizable changes to their overall culture to create an inclusive and equitable workplace. If diverse staff don't feel safe pointing out problematic tech, or aren't supported when they do, how is diversity alone going to solve the problem?

The current reality is that those who broach topics of diversity are often ignored or punished by company leadership; a 2016 research paper in the *Academy of Management Journal* found that women and nonwhite employees who promote diversity are penalized with lower performance ratings (http://bkaprt. com/dfs37/05-04). While many people do bravely point out problems with a company's products and issues within their workplace, others cannot risk losing their employment in order to take a stand. For diversity to be a tool against harmful tech, employees from marginalized groups must feel safe to share their ideas and concerns as well as be supported when they push back against the status quo.

Another problem with the idea that diversity can fix oppressive tech is the expectation that people who have experienced trauma, either due to belonging to a certain demographic (race, gender, sexual orientation) or due to life experiences (rape, child abuse, mental illness), should willingly share their trauma with their teams in the workplace in an effort to make their product more inclusive. Ideally, workplaces would be safe and supportive enough to make this sort of sharing the norm; but this is rarely the case, and creating trauma-informed and equitable organizations requires serious investment and large shifts in workplace culture.

While adding more diverse identities to a team is a good start, it doesn't equal more diverse decision-making power. We need to push harder to make workplaces inclusive of historically excluded groups, including efforts to retain and promote people from those groups into positions of authority. When we consider, for example, that Apple's overall workforce (including nontechnical workers) is 9 percent Black, but the number falls to 3 percent when looking at leadership roles, it's clear that the dominant groups are still hoarding power (http://bkaprt.com/dfs37/05-05).

This incomplete approach to diversity, equity, and inclusion (DEI) work, which only emphasizes the "diversity" part, results in "snowcapped" companies: employees of color are grouped at the bottom of the hierarchy, with little institutional influence, while those with the power, who are more likely to be white, sit at the top (like a snowcapped mountain). For diversity to be part of the solution to unethical tech, it's not enough to hire people from historically and currently excluded groups into junior roles; white leadership must intentionally choose to share or give power to employees of color by promoting them into leadership positions and ensuring they have the necessary authority to successfully work against harmful tech.

We should all be working hard toward a more diverse, inclusive, and equitable tech field—including the many larger, systemic-level changes required for people from historically excluded groups to successfully do the work of fixing broken tech. But if we want diversity to be the fix some believe it to be, it must be paired with the essential work of creating inclusive and equitable workplaces.

## TUNING IN TO HARMFUL SITUATIONS

Ultimately, no single factor can guarantee that our tech will never cause harm or be weaponized for violence. The Process for Inclusive Safety is meant to give teams the time and tools to identify how their products might enable abuse so they can take appropriate steps to either prevent that abuse or ensure that victims can quickly understand what's going on and regain some amount of power. Even after going through the Process, you should be on high alert for user-reported instances of harm and be ready to quickly course-correct.

The Process for Inclusive Safety is just one part in the overall effort to create a tech landscape that prioritizes safety. Ideally, if companies can get on board with efforts like this to keep their users safe, they'll already be making a concerted effort to make their workplace safe for groups that have been historically marginalized and excluded from product discussions.

# 6 RESEARCHING SAFETY CONCERNS

WHEN DOING ANY KIND of research, you can safely assume that some of your participants will have survived trauma. This means that when doing safety-focused design research, where you'll be specifically discussing the potential harms you've identified, the chances of retraumatizing someone are high.

An intentional approach and careful education are key to preventing harm to your participants. Doing this sort of research can also be difficult for researchers, who need to understand their own limits and put practices in place to reduce the chance of burnout and vicarious trauma.

Researching safety is a sensitive undertaking and requires us to be highly empathetic, while also recognizing that our empathy is not a stand-in for lived experience. This chapter will help you add some specialized tools to your standard research toolkit that help people on both sides of the research remain safe.

# THE LIMITS OF EMPATHY

A few years ago, I redesigned a data input interface that had been made up of multiple portals, each with their own tedious steps. During my research, I got to know the employee who handled the majority of the data input. She was stressed out by the interface's many intricacies, which made it difficult to avoid mistakes. Seeing the interface for myself, I could empathize: it prompted for information in a different order than she received it, was so detailed that it was overwhelming to look at, and required the use of both keyboard and mouse, which made it tiring.

I redesigned the interface so that she could enter the data in the order she received it, chunked it into smaller sections to make it less overwhelming, and ensured it could be navigated through tabbing, since she preferred using a keyboard to a mouse. I was able to use empathy to design a stronger product in this case because the empathizing was about her work, not about her identities.

In contrast, no matter how strongly I empathize, I, as white person, can never understand firsthand the experience of racism that Black people experience in the US. If I worked at Airbnb and were on a team working to reduce the negative experiences of Black people using the platform, it would be inappropriate for me to interview Black people about their life experiences and then assume I could speak on their behalf, or to decide how Airbnb should function for Black people.

The same holds true for people whose experience with trauma is relevant to the design process, such as survivors of sexual assault or domestic violence: we can't pretend that our empathy is as good as having lived those experiences ourselves. Empathy is not a stand-in for representation.

The solution, then, is to recognize when our empathy has reached its limits and include people from the necessary groups in the design process (and pay them for sharing their lived experiences and knowledge). If the product is specifically for a certain group, such as domestic violence survivors, we need to pay real survivors to give their knowledge during the research phase and to participate in the design process—and share ownership and accountability over the product (I'll talk more about that in Chapter 7).

We should all try to empathize with others. Empathy is enormously important to being a good designer. But it should only inform our work in non-identity-bearing ways; when it comes to designing for different identities, people from those groups need to be included in the process and represent themselves rather than being represented by a designer who empathizes with them.

## INTERVIEWING VULNERABLE USERS

Interviewing vulnerable groups requires special preparation and consideration and may not always follow the same guidance you've learned for doing more general user research. Let's walk through some important details you'll want to nail down when undertaking user research of this nature.

### Self-education

Before doing research with a sensitive group, do everything you can to learn about their particular type of trauma. Do general research online and look for work from current experts and activists working in that particular space. Many activists run accounts on Twitter and Instagram that are great for learning about specific types of oppression and sensitive topics—Googling "best Instagram accounts for fat activism" (or whatever you're researching) is a good place to start.

Whenever possible, interview experts at nonprofits and other groups who serve the population. This minimizes the possibility of an interviewee having to educate you about the general facts of their personal trauma, as it can reinforce the feeling of isolation and the upsetting idea that their experiences are abnormal or misunderstood.

## Finding participants

One of the best ways to find participants to interview about a particular trauma is to work with nonprofits and other groups focused on serving that population. Working with these experts can also help ensure that you are conducting your research in a sensitive manner; whenever possible, ask for help from experts in crafting your surveys and interview questions, get feedback, and learn from the experts about how to properly work with the target population.

## Preinterview dialogue

Before beginning an interview, most researchers share some information with the interviewee to give them context, put them at ease, and build trust. This usually includes telling them that they don't need to share anything they don't feel comfortable with, that their responses will be anonymized, and that the contents of the interview will only be shared with the research team.

These basics are doubly important when working with survivors of trauma. In addition to your standard preinterview dialogue, make sure you:

- Assign interviewees a fake name to better ensure anonymity.
- Ask for permission to take notes or record the interview.
- Verbalize that you really appreciate them sharing their experience.
- Remind them what your work is about.
- Tell them everything you will do with their data, how you are protecting it, and who will see it.

I have found that people are more interested in sharing their traumatic experiences when they know doing so will help others in similar situations, so be sure to directly connect the fact that this interview will help others by making your product safer.

Additionally, take care not to pressure respondents to self-identify as a "survivor" or other term. Many people who have survived traumatic experiences don't like the various labels that get applied to them. If a participant uses a term such as "survivor" or "victim" or "former addict" to describe themselves, follow their lead and use that term, but don't be the first one to apply the term to them. You'll likely have to use a term when describing the project and the interview ("we're creating an app for managing finances and are interviewing domestic violence survivors to understand the risks of financial abuse"), but don't apply a certain term to them until they've made it clear which term they prefer.

As a general rule, never pressure participants to share personal trauma that they don't want to share. The trust and rapport that researchers seek to build with interview subjects should not be violated in order to procure stories of trauma and abuse. Tell the interviewee they don't have to answer anything they're uncomfortable with and that they can stop the interview at any time—and follow through on those promises.

## Writing questions

When writing questions for surveys and interviews, frame questions in a way that allows the interviewee to anonymize their story if they wish. Even if you're interviewing someone specifically because of their lived experience, such as someone recovering from a substance abuse disorder or a sexual assault survivor, participants may still wish to convey certain stories or details as if they happened to a friend. This isn't in line with typical UX research methods, but it's an appropriate tactic for protecting your research subjects while still eliciting important stories.

For example, if I were creating a feature for a shared online bank account, instead of asking the interviewee, "Have you ever had someone you share a bank account with restrict access to your money?" I'd say, "We've found in our research that there can be issues with shared bank accounts where one person controls the other person's access to the account and the money in it. Have you ever had anything like this happen to you, or known someone this happened to?" This gives them the chance to tell their own story of abuse as though it happened to someone else, as well as share actual stories of others. (Note that if they use a name, this should also be anonymized.)

Just like with standard research questions, avoid leading questions. Don't use words like "abuse," "harass," "torment," or "monitor." Not only are these words leading, but many survivors don't always classify their experiences as "abuse." It's not our job to force that term onto their experiences.

## Managing your reaction

You will hear traumatic stories through this research. Although it can be difficult, it's important to keep your composure. You're not a therapist or a friend. Don't cry or become overly emotional, as this can cause the interviewee to feel like they need to take care of you in that moment. If you're like me, you may need to cry or swear loudly and angrily after hearing a particularly intense or sad story; do everything in your power to wait until the interview is over to release your emotions.

During my interviews with survivors of domestic violence, the most reaction I give is a slight facial expression, such as raising my eyebrows in surprise and sometimes giving a quiet "wow" or "dang" to show that I'm actively listening and appreciate the intensity of the experience the interviewee is sharing with me.

Before you conduct any interviews, plan how you'll respond to difficult stories when they're over. Thank the interviewee for sharing their experience and say something to acknowledge the seriousness of what they went through, such as:

- "Thank you for sharing this. I'm so glad you're safe now."
- "I really appreciate you sharing your story, and I'm really glad things are better now."
- "Thank you so much for sharing your experience; it's incredibly helpful."

## Safe remote interviewing

Remote interviewing comes with some special considerations when doing research with vulnerable groups. If possible, postpone the interview until it's safe to do it in person. If it's not possible, proceed to remote interviews with caution.

Unlike in-person interviewing, remote interviewing does not ensure privacy and confidentiality for the person being interviewed. Some participants may not want other people in the home to overhear their experiences with topics such as surviving a war or sexual assault. People experiencing domestic violence who are still living with their abuser won't be as likely to share relevant information due to the risk of being overheard.

Attempt to schedule remote interviews at a time when the interviewee will be home alone. Because an interviewee's email may not be private, instead of saying outright that you may be discussing sensitive topics they might not want others to overhear, you can allude to it indirectly with something like: "If possible, we'd like to do the interview while you are home alone to ensure we aren't disturbed."

During the interview, ask the interviewee if they are in a private space where they cannot be disturbed. If there is a possibility of being overheard, the interviewer should not ask questions about domestic violence, as this could jeopardize the interviewee's safety.

The Sexual Violence Research Initiative, which focuses on gathering, analyzing, and disseminating information about violence against women and children, created a useful guide to conducting remote research sessions during the COVID-19 pandemic. The guide includes a handy table of attributes researchers should consider when employing various methods of virtual data collection (FIG 6) (http://bkaprt.com/dfs37/06-01, PDF).

Other key best practices for remote interviewing include:

- Use a service that blocks the researcher's number when making calls to people's personal phones. This protects the researcher from unwanted contact from research participants or others who have access to their phone.

| ATTRIBUTES | VIDEO CALL (Zoom, Skype, FaceTime, WhatsApp, etc.) | AUDIO CALL (mobile or fixed-line phone) | INTERACTIVE VOICE RESPONSE (automated phone survey) | PHONE-BASED SURVEY (SMS, WhatsApp) | ONLINE SURVEY (Survey Monkey, etc.) |
|---|---|---|---|---|---|
| Self-administered | | | X | X | X |
| Interviewer administered | X | X | | | |
| Requires internet access via smartphone/tablet/laptop | X | | | | X |
| Requires literacy | | | | X | X |
| Requires IT-literacy | X | | | | X |
| Requires researcher training | X | X | | | |
| Ability to probe/ask follow-up questions | X | X | | | |
| Ability to address participant concerns immediately | X | X | | | |
| Easily reach large number of participants in diverse geographic areas | | | X | X | X |
| High flexibility (participants can respond on their own time) | | | X | X | X |
| May improve social desirability bias/accurate disclosures | | | X | X | X |
| Data trail/high security concerns | X | | X | X | X |
| Privacy, confidentiality and other safety risks | X | X | X | X | X |

FIG 6: There are many considerations to make when it comes to various forms of remote research, as summarized by this table from the Sexual Violence Research Initiative.

- Build trust quickly in the conversation and establish a non-judgmental tone. Interviewees may need prompts from you to help vocalize if they are feeling uncomfortable or need to end the interview for a safety reason.
- Pay special attention to prolonged silences, shifts in tone, and new background noises. When you notice these sorts of changes, you should check again to make sure it's safe to keep going by asking things like, "Is this still a good environment for this interview?" or "Is it okay for us to continue, or would you like to pause here and pick this up again later?"

Finally, recognize that remote interviewing, like all remote work, can be more taxing for the interviewers. Plan to take breaks more frequently.

# COPING WITH VICARIOUS TRAUMA

Vicarious trauma, or indirect trauma, is trauma that happens from witnessing or hearing about the traumatic experiences of others. It's common among victim services professionals and emergency medical professionals and is a possible outcome of doing the research necessary to design for safety.

Vicarious trauma is more likely if your research lasts a long time, and can lead to burnout, stress, and compassion fatigue (physical, emotional, and spiritual depletion). The following practices can help combat vicarious trauma and help ensure that designing for safety doesn't impact your own mental wellness. If you're a team of one, you will need to work hard to recognize your limits and put the following practices into place; if you're part of a team, the team lead should regularly promote these tactics. (The following practices are also useful for researchers who are survivors of the particular trauma being researched and might be triggered by the interviews. These teammates should be especially aware of their ability to conduct research without being re-traumatized, and either opt out of or discontinue participating in the research if it becomes overwhelming).

## Establish boundaries

Establishing boundaries means you recognize when you're hitting your breaking point and taking a step back. On teams, instead of having one person do all the interviews, divide them among team members to reduce exposure. Plan breaks between interviews so that you can have a day or two off from interviewing to recover before doing more. Establish these schedules before undertaking research into a sensitive topic so you build in the time you need.

## Practice self-care

Despite what capitalism and consumerism would have us think, self-care is not just bubble baths and face masks. Self-care means doing what you need to do to have a true break and recover some peace for yourself. For me, self-care is petting my dogs and rereading my favorite novels. For someone else it might be an afternoon of ordering Chipotle and indulging in an entire season of *The Office*. Others may need hiking and fresh air, going for a quiet drive, or knitting while listening to podcasts. Figure out what helps you rest and recharge, and build time in your schedule to do it regularly while you're doing emotionally heavy research.

## Utilize therapy

I cannot overstate the importance of therapy when doing trauma research. You don't need to wait for a crisis to get started. If you have access to mental health services, find a therapist you like and see them regularly. Remote therapy has become much easier to find (as well as more prevalent) due to the COVID-19 pandemic, which also prompted a surge in adjacent solutions such as therapy apps, guided meditations, and wellness programs. It's becoming more common for employers to comp services like these for their employees. Larger companies often also have (but may not widely advertise) employee assistance programs (EAPs), whose services include helping employees get access to a limited number of therapy sessions as well as help with financial and legal concerns. In short, identify a strong support system for yourself—even vicarious trauma carries serious impact, and there may be more resources available to you than you know.

## BE INTENTIONAL

When doing research with sensitive groups, intentionality is key. Be intentional about not exploiting and retraumatizing interviewees; be intentional about self-care and counter-acting vicarious trauma; be intentional about your game plan for remote interviewing. This sort of research is too important to leave anything up to chance.

So far, this book has focused on designing products and services with the safety of vulnerable groups in mind, and this chapter covered how to research sensitive issues and ensure you don't retraumatize research participants. But what about designing products that are specifically *for* those subsets of users? The next chapter will cover how to approach a project that's distinctly for groups that are vulnerable or have survived traumatic experiences.

# TECH FOR VULNERABLE GROUPS

LET'S BEGIN WITH THE cautionary tale of the Aspire News app. Backed by Dr. Phil and his wife Robin McGraw, Aspire News is intended to help people experiencing domestic violence. It's disguised as a news app and enables users to send alerts to contacts asking for help, access articles about domestic violence, and get further support from a list of hotlines.

While these are all useful features, the app is rife with problems. In 2020, a pair of security researchers found it was easy to access the personal recordings users made to send to their contacts during a moment of danger. The URLs used to access the recordings were not secure, and simply shortening the URLs allowed the researchers to access any users' recordings—a security lapse anyone could use to identify users experiencing domestic violence, putting them in further danger (http://bkaprt.com/dfs37/07-01).

Additionally, core features of the app simply don't work. When I looked into the app's details in the App Store in late 2020, the reviews were filled with users reporting bugs and unsafe features:

- "As someone who is in a verbal abusive relationship the app will get me in trouble. Here's the thing, love how there's new stories to make this app look like I'm reading about the news. However, when I go to the Get Education section to learn about abuse and steps, the links link out to my web browser automatically instead of being inside the app...So then I have to clear my history browser. C'mon, if you're creating something to keep women safe, don't have it link out! Everything should be in the app." (It appears this problem, at least, has been rectified—when I used the app, the articles opened within it, not a separate browser.)
- "Thank God I did not rely on this app for its intended purposes. No content, majority of the tabs do not respond when selected. Had I needed immediate help...I would have been caught."
- "I tested the emergency triple tap thing and it only worked one time (out of the 5 or 6 times I tried!) to one contact (rather than both contacts I entered). It tends to freeze as well."
- "I work in the Victim Services field and would like to use this as a Safety Plan resource. In testing, I could only get it to send the message intermittently and it always got the location wrong. Also, it would be very easy for an abuser to get into the "settings" in the app and figure out just what it is."

One user reported that all the news stories in the app were from left-leaning sources, which would make a right-leaning user less able to disguise the app as a realistic news source. When I downloaded the app in late 2020, I found that there were no news stories in any of the categories, only a message saying, "There are no articles yet. Check back in a bit."

The various design and performance issues with the Aspire News app add up to a product with good intentions but harmful and dangerous impacts that are likely to hurt the very people it intends to help.

Creating tech that is specifically *for* a vulnerable and/or traumatized group is an area with little formal direction. The story of the Aspire News app highlights just one instance of technologists thinking they're equipped to take on designing a product for a sensitive population, only to end up endangering that population more. Good intentions are worthless in the face of harmful impacts. When it comes to tech meant specifically for vulnerable or traumatized groups, thoughtful design and robust testing are vital to keeping users safe.

In this chapter, I'm attempting to bring the principles of designing for safety together with the knowledge of design justice and trauma-informed design advocates. I hope to impress upon readers the special considerations around taking on these kinds of projects as well as the risks of getting it wrong. We'll revisit some aspects of the Aspire News story later in this chapter, as it's a useful example we can learn from. But first, let's walk through the basic principles of trauma-informed design.

## TRAUMA-INFORMED DESIGN

Designers creating tech for vulnerable groups who have experienced trauma must prioritize trauma-informed design. In tech, trauma-informed design means designing our products in a way that does not retraumatize vulnerable populations. The primary source of guidance in this space comes from designer Theresa Slate, who draws from the field of trauma-informed care (used primarily in health care) and expands these best practices to the tech space. Slate presented a set of trauma-informed design principles during a public UXPA (User Experience Professionals' Association) course I attended—these five principles are a great starting point.

1.  **Prioritize comfort over technological trends.** Users should understand what's coming as opposed to being surprised by changes in the design. Ideally this education should happen ahead of time, and users should be able to choose when they enter into the new or updated design so that they can do so when they're comfortable. Give warnings about new integrations, and be honest about both the benefits and potential downsides of any new features.
2.  **Make informed consent a requirement, not a nice-to-have.** Users must be fully informed in order to give authentic consent, which means resisting the urge to assume that a

lack of a "no" is the same as a "yes." For example, don't opt people into receiving promotional updates by default, and avoid complex legalese when writing terms and conditions.

3. **Build partnerships, not user bases.** Whenever possible, allow people to have a say in their experiences through customization. Designers should also solicit feedback from users, especially the most critical ones. Respond to user feedback in a meaningful way rather than deferring to an automated response that doesn't include follow up.

4. **Measure transparency over conversion.** Conversion metrics measure movement, but not comprehension. One way to check if users are confused by a product is to tag customer support calls and set goals around reducing the call load related to product confusion.

5. **Lead with respect, not superiority.** Design education often teaches us that we as designers have the tools to uncover all the answers to our users' problems. Instead, designers should aim to work in partnership with the communities our products serve.

These principles will give you a foundation for taking on this type of work, but you'll still have to exercise caution and work thoroughly. Creating a product specifically for vulnerable groups is not something to be taken on lightly. You can expect to spend more time on research and testing than you would on a typical product. Be prepared to make a large commitment in terms of time and money.

## CENTERING THE IMPACTED COMMUNITY

When creating a product specifically for a vulnerable or traumatized population, that population must be at the center of every decision. The impacted community is the most important stakeholder, and their needs and goals are the product's priorities. Centering the impacted community means making a long-term investment in the product's success and doing careful research, as well as giving the community ownership over the process and its outcomes, and working with them on the solutions they have already defined.

## Existing solutions over quick fixes

Creating tech for sensitive groups means making a commitment in terms of both time and power. Too often, well-meaning tech companies that want to help solve a problem "parachute" into the community from the outside, fail to understand already-existing solutions, and deliver a quick fix of their own design—only to leave before the implications and outcomes of the solution are fully understood. Companies making tech for vulnerable or traumatized groups must instead commit to a long-term investment that includes working with the impacted group on a solution, sticking around to understand the solution's effectiveness, and continuing to iterate.

In *Design Justice* (required reading for this field), designer and communications scholar Sasha Costanza-Chock explains, "Wherever people face challenges, they are always already working to deal with those challenges; wherever a community is oppressed, they are always already developing strategies to resist oppression." They suggest designers creating products specifically for these communities ask how design "can best be used as a tool to amplify, support, and extend existing community-based processes" (http://bkaprt.com/dfs37/07-02).

People, including those in marginalized or vulnerable situations, are experts in their own problems, and are already working on answers to deal with them. Designers should magnify and reinforce those solutions.

## Define your users carefully

Groups that are marginalized in our society are also marginalized with regard to how support services respond to their issues. Rather than treating the vulnerable group as a monolith with the same experiences, designers should take care to identify and understand these differences so that the solutions they build actually cater to the full range of users. The research phase of your design process should include an intersectional analysis when designing tech for vulnerable groups.

Intersectionality refers to the cumulative ways that multiple forms of discrimination (such as racism, sexism, and ageism) combine, overlap, and intersect. For example, a Black woman will face both sexism as a woman, and racism as a Black person, creating an experience of oppression that is unique to Black women.

The term was coined by Black feminist scholar Kimberlé Williams Crenshaw in 1989, who wrote that "the intersectional experience is greater than the sum of racism and sexism." Considering intersectionality in the tech we build for vulnerable groups is vitally important. When we don't, we make broad assumptions about what a seemingly specific user group needs and risk excluding people who don't fit the dominant cultural narratives of vulnerability. For example:

- Users with accessibility needs, such as those who are blind or have low vision, are physically disabled, or have a chronic illness, are often left out of narrowly defined groups.
- Apps serving domestic violence survivors often exclude male users and queer users.
- Women cannot be lumped together in a single category; factors like race, age, and immigration status must be considered. For example, Black women are more likely to face hostility from responding police officers when reporting a crime, meaning it should not be assumed that all women will feel the same way about reporting a crime to law enforcement.

Designing for domestic violence survivors demands we understand how their experiences vary among women, men, queer people, and people of color (also not a monolith—consider the different experiences among Black, Latinx, Indigenous, and Asian groups). How do these groups process trauma differently? How do they look for support? Thoughtful research will help you answer these questions.

## Give the community control

Most designers, including me, were trained to treat users as something like test subjects. They're crucial to research but aren't stakeholders. We might invite them to a "design thinking workshop" to extract ideas about how to design solutions for the problems our research identified. When the product launches, they're invited to buy into it; sometimes for a "free" exchange of demographic information (data which, naturally, the product designers will own) or for actual money.

When designing a product specifically for a marginalized group, the extractive nature of this process is exploitative, unethical, and unjust. In *Design Justice*, Costanza-Chock points out that current best practices around including users in the design process say nothing about who receives credit for the product, ownership over it, and a share of profits that it might generate.

This kind of inclusion becomes possible when we involve members of our target group in every step of the process, and share control over the outcomes, such as information or revenue generated by the product. It's ethically questionable, at best, to profit off a product that solves an essential problem faced by a marginalized group, and the skewed priorities may even cause new kinds of harm to an already-vulnerable part of the population.

Additionally, the end product is much more likely to be effective at solving a group's problems if that group is fully involved in the process. Costanza-Chock writes that "justice demands" that designers include members of the community who will be most impacted by the final product in the design process: "the tacit and experiential knowledge of community members is sure to produce ideas, approaches, and innovations that a nonmember of the community would be extremely unlikely to come up with."

Ultimately, truly centering the community a piece of tech is intended to help means giving that community control over the design process and its outcomes.

# DESIGNING FOR SAFETY

As we've seen, products aimed at helping a vulnerable, traumatized, or marginalized group should be approached with care. Designers should understand the risks of their product doing more harm than good, approach research with an intersectional lens, take the time to thoroughly educate themselves, and create a plan that involves working closely with advocates and survivors. If time and space cannot be made to invest in these tasks, your team should carefully consider if they are the right people to be taking on this project.

The stakes with products like these are high, and designers should not enter into these sorts of projects lightly. As discussed in Chapter 1, good intent doesn't erase harmful impacts, and if the product has the potential to inadvertently expose the user to more harm than if they hadn't used the product, it must be designed with more caution than the typical tech product.

## Get educated about justice and trauma

Technologists taking on projects specifically for helping sensitive groups are obliged to understand the role of justice within their work and need to understand trauma and its impact. I've already mentioned *Design Justice* by Sasha Costanza-Chock, which is a superb book that explores the relationship between power, design, and social justice. I also recommend *The Body Keeps the Score* by Bessel van der Kolk, which thoroughly details the pervasiveness of trauma and its impact on the body and brain.

Whatever issue your product is focused on, find the experts in that field, and read their work.

## Work with survivors and their advocates

Remember the limits of empathy: no amount of research or empathizing can replace lived experiences. Designers taking on a project specifically for a sensitive group should be especially intentional about working hand in hand with experts and survivors who have experience with the issue. It's always a good idea to work *with* users rather than *for* users; when designing specifically for these groups, it's essential.

Leonie Tanczer is the principal investigator of the Gender and IoT project at University College London, which examines the relationship between IoT technology and gender-based domestic violence (http://bkaprt.com/dfs37/07-03). Tanczer reiterates that IoT and other tech initiatives must include specialists who work with survivors, are trauma-informed, and understand how to do victim risk assessments and safety planning. Those are the people who are equipped to solve this problem, she says; we cannot rely on a "corporation that believes their new feature or app could help save the world." (http://bkaprt. com/dfs37/01-03).

While tech solutions can be enormously valuable to people in dangerous or vulnerable situations, we must always work with people with the proper lived experience and their advocates to inform those products.

## Perform rigorous quality assurance testing

While bugs in a new app are forgivable, the stakes are so high in apps meant for vulnerable populations that we can't overlook robust testing and quality assurance before releasing them. Thoroughly test features that are aimed at improving the safety or mental well-being of sensitive groups to ensure they function as expected across all devices and browsers.

Additionally, take special care with the design and functionality to accommodate situations where a phone may be offline or experiencing a slow connection. Users should always understand exactly what the app is capable of in the moment they're using it and be able to quickly grasp if certain features are not available.

## Provide help safely

It is key to remember that these products are often for people living in very dangerous contexts. All content, copy, and information that make up digital experiences need to take that context into account. For example, the Aspire News app initially opened articles about domestic violence in the browser rather than within the app, which was a dangerous design, as abusers often monitor their victims' mobile device browser history. Had the design been informed by survivors who knew these dangers, they might not have made the mistake of loading articles in the browser and would have kept the user in the app. An additional proactive step might have clarified this within the app: "Any links you click will load in the Aspire app and won't be saved to your browser history."

When someone inadvertently alerts their abuser that they are researching domestic violence and resources for leaving the relationship, this can cause further harm and increased monitoring. Consider the unique ecosystem of your product, and design it as carefully as possible to avoid this worst-case scenario for people in vulnerable situations.

## Don't make assumptions

It's always important to allow the user to consent to using certain features, but it's absolutely vital when it comes to features designed to support them during a dangerous time. We cannot make assumptions about what's physically or psychologically safe for them to do—nor should we assume that they're helpless.

Developers of apps and products that aim to offer proactive support need to tread carefully here, as we discussed in Chapter 5 where we used the example of a pregnancy app that allowed the user to report that they were the victim of an assault. Even if it seems obvious to app developers that such users need to be connected with domestic violence resources, it needs to be the user's decision to opt in to receiving that information. Automatically connecting them to those services without clear consent would be an overstep; all the app should do is ask the question and let the user determine their path from there.

Similarly, designers must question their own beliefs about the concept at hand, such as the idea that survivors of violence (or anyone) will want to engage with law enforcement. When it comes to designing products for sensitive groups, every foundational fact that seems to be a given must be researched and validated.

Some users experiencing domestic violence may already know full well they're in an abusive relationship, and don't want to receive support. Some may already be receiving support and be in the process of safely leaving. Others may decline support because their abuser is monitoring them through spyware that allows them to see activity on the phone's screen or may have device syncing set up that allows them to see the victim's activity on their own device. Support should be offered to users but never forced on them.

## PROCEED WITH CAUTION AND CARE

When a piece of tech is meant to help a marginalized, traumatized, or vulnerable community, we need to take special care—both to keep the community safe, and to authentically include the community in the work. It's unethical to extract their knowledge and ideas for profit. (Repeat this to any unscrupulous stakeholders until it sinks in.) As the Aspire News app shows, working hand in hand with the impacted community is absolutely vital.

You've probably noticed that so far, this book has contained many, many specific design solutions for combating the problem of unsafe tech. But as I said in Chapter 5, individuals alone cannot fix institutional problems—and we are facing many institutional problems when it comes to unethical, unsafe tech. Solving them will require changes at an individual and team level (the solutions provided so far) as well as at a larger, systemic level. The final chapter offers ideas for the necessary large-scale changes needed to create a paradigm shift for safe and ethical tech.

# 8 PROACTIVE SUPPORT AND FUTURE WORK

IN 2020, ON REDDIT's "Am I the Asshole?" (AITA) board, a woman shared that her husband had spent money she'd been saving for a pain-relieving surgery (http://bkaprt.com/dfs37/08-01). She explained that she and her husband had been planning the surgery for years, putting money into a savings account on which both were listed as owners, "but it was never linked to my online banking." In yet another instance of banking software making financial abuse all too easy, her husband had secretly withdrawn the $15,000 in the account, which she only found out about when she called the bank.

The Reddit users who responded to her post assured her she was "not the asshole" for wanting the surgery and being angry about the missing money—and many explained that what her husband had done was both physically and financially abusive. Having hundreds or even thousands of strangers confirm that an experience constitutes abuse can be a powerful experience for survivors, who often update their posts to say that they have finally realized they were being abused and have separated from their partner.

Although AITA doesn't allow situations that clearly depict violence, it receives so many submissions that involve descriptions of nonphysical domestic abuse that moderators created a post titled "New Resources for Anyone Looking to Help Those in an Unhealthy or Abusive Relationship," which was pinned to the top of the board for several months (http://bkaprt.com/dfs37/08-02).

Adding a post that directly addresses domestic violence is an example of using technology to offer meaningful support to users experiencing abuse. This is what's possible when designers acknowledge the reality of their users and take proactive steps to help them.

## A PARADIGM SHIFT TO SAFETY DESIGN

The focus of this book so far has been to help you understand how tech is weaponized for abuse, and how individual technologists and teams can take specific actions to increase product safety. But what if we went further than simply preventing harm? What if we were able to recognize when our users were in a harmful or dangerous situation and proactively offer support? What needs to change to make designing for safety the norm?

In order for designing for safety to become standard practice, we need large, systemic shifts in how we consider safety and ethics in tech. When we bring together individual and team-level efforts with wider changes in our companies and institutions, we can begin to create a paradigm shift away from unsafe, uncaring, unethical tech and toward a technology industry that prioritizes safety, inclusion, and compassion.

That said, our current tech landscape is grim: government oversight remains laughable, and the tech industry offers enormous profits with no consequences for bad behavior. We've watched as Mark Zuckerberg has shown us how a massively powerful tech company like Facebook can do harm—enabling cyberbullying, allowing misinformation to spread like wildfire, and literally undermining democracy and contributing to genocide. And each time the company faces public outrage, he merely issues an apology, pledges to do better, and then continues to do exactly the same terrible things as before (http://bkaprt.com/dfs37/08-03).

The individuals who choose to work toward safe, just, and inclusive tech are fighting an industry standard that places profits over the safety of people. In his limited-run *New York Times* newsletter *The Privacy Project*, Charlie Warzel explained how industry leaders justify their bad actions with the notion that "this couldn't be wrong because it's the industry standard" (http://bkaprt.com/dfs37/08-04).

The idea that it's alright to do whatever unethical thing is currently the industry norm is widespread in tech, and dangerous. It's led to children being bullied on social media to the point that they die by suicide. It's allowed vengeful abusers to track down and murder their victims. It's led to a misinformation crisis that spans our country's vaccine efforts to our election processes.

While some companies do choose to prioritize safety, for most it's an afterthought, with perhaps a few rank-and-file employees pushing—with mixed success rates and the occasional major win—for changes to make their product more inclusive and safer.

This is why individual action alone will never make tech safe and ethical. Any approach that relies on individuals who opt in to doing the work and ignores the institutions that perpetuate harm will fail to achieve the large-scale transformation we need. We need both individual action and groups of individuals pushing our company leadership and government officials to make safety in tech a norm.

## CHANGE AT EVERY LEVEL

Changing the systems and institutions that we work within will require evolution at various touchpoints within them. We need to start with education, instilling concepts of safety and ethics in the students who will one day become technologists. And once those workers are inside tech companies, they need to belong to unions who will not only protect their rights as employees but give institutional backing to the time we need to design for safe, inclusive, and ethical products.

## Start at the beginning

I'd love to see every tech-oriented educational space incorporate designing for safety into their curricula: bootcamps, university courses, and online self-study programs. We want to reach technologists before they've even entered the field. Students can train early on tech misuse and abuse and learn practical methods for identifying and preventing issues of safety, security, and marginalization.

Every group in the tech space can make better, safer products with this information—not just designers, but also developers, project managers, data scientists, and QA analysts. Including safety, inclusivity, and ethics in the learning journey of every future technologist will prepare them to do this work starting on day one at their first jobs, as well as normalize the need for this work, which plays a part in the second level where change is needed: tech unions.

## Standardize safe design

Unions, in essence, bring employees together as an organized group with collective power. That power translates into bargaining with employers for better wages, benefits, and working conditions. And just because tech workers are, at this moment, generally well-paid compared to other industries doesn't mean we shouldn't have unions; things being good now is no guarantee that things will remain good. Unions help ensure that the things employees love about a company aren't subjected to the whims of the CEO, that wages and benefits are distributed equally among workers, and that employees who are let go are treated with dignity and get enough of a cushion to survive the immediate aftermath of a firing.

When it comes to creating safe and ethical tech, unions are our best bet for transforming personal standards for design work—like those I've covered here about designing for safety—

into industry standards that get the backing of formal policy and make doing this work the norm. It won't matter how quickly a VP wants to move on a project or what the budget is for a new feature. With the support of a union, individual designers wouldn't need to individually shoulder the work of convincing stakeholders to prioritize things like diversity, inclusion, ethical tech and designing for safety; it simply becomes another part of the spec.

### Don't put the burden on workers

Pressuring individuals to put their jobs on the line so they can advocate for safe and inclusive tech is both unfair and ineffective. A few years ago, I pushed for a corporate client to include gender options beyond simply "male" and "female" for their users. This effort was moderately successful, as I was able to bring my immediate stakeholder on board, who escalated the request up the complex chain of command, where it got stuck in debates about the database implications the change would have. This went on for months, and eventually the project ended, and I moved onto a new client.

In this situation, what's an ethical designer to do? Quitting your job on principle is a privilege; those without work lined up, or enough wealth saved up to go without income for a time, cannot simply leave. Instead of asking individuals to figure out how to make taking a stand for ethical tech work with their financial situation, the ideal solution is something else entirely: the backing of professional standards and legislation that mandate safe and inclusive tech as well as broader changes such as healthcare reform.

No tech employee should have to go through the ethical dilemmas that we regularly go through right now, with the specter of unemployment, loss of health care, and all that can follow hanging over our heads. If we had an established set of standards that we as practitioners of this discipline had to follow, and if those standards came from a legal policy with teeth behind it, the burden would be lifted on us as individuals. As it turns out, the fight for ethical tech is intimately entwined with the fight for basic human rights such as housing and health care.

If we could rest assured that losing our jobs wouldn't result in lack of access to those needs, we'd be better equipped to take a principled stand.

Laws are never ahead of the curve; they're a cap on an enormous amount of work on the part of activists, academics, and everyday workers who lay the foundation by challenging harmful systems and proposing innovative solutions. People who are happy with the status quo typically label these solutions as "too radical" to warrant serious consideration. That's where we are now. But history tells us that with enough work, we can make massive paradigm shifts and create new norms for the role of technology in our society.

## THE NEED FOR REGULATION

The story of the seat belt is highly instructive here. Seat belts reduce serious injuries and fatalities in car crashes by half, but when they were first introduced in the mid-1950s, amid skyrocketing auto fatalities, no one wanted them.

Part of the problem was that they were an add-on feature that drivers could only purchase for an additional cost. In 1956, when the "seat belt option" was an extra $27 (which is around $250 now), only 2 percent of Ford buyers opted to buy them, and auto fatalities continued to be unnecessarily high (http://bkaprt.com/dfs37/08-05).

In 1965, Ralph Nader (the same Ralph Nader who later ran for president multiple times with the Green Party) wrote an exposé about how car manufacturers were prioritizing profits over the safety of their users. What followed was one of the most successful public health campaigns of all time. Nader's investigation led to Congress creating what would become the National Highway Traffic Safety Administration (NHTSA), and a new law requiring all vehicles (except buses) to be fitted with seat belts (http://bkaprt.com/dfs37/08-06).

But the law didn't fix everything: After it passed and seat belts came as a standard part of new cars instead of at an additional cost, people were still against them. In 1983, less than 15 percent of Americans were buckling up consistently (http://

bkaprt.com/dfs37/08-07). In an effort to change this, New York became the first state to require occupants to wear seat belts in 1984, and the rest of the states followed suit throughout the 1980s and '90s. The exception is New Hampshire, the Live Free or Die state, which only requires children to be belted; adults can do as they wish, and many choose not to.

New Hampshire aside, the state laws encouraged norms to shift, and over the following decades children grew up with the habit of wearing them. Seat belts are now widely used, with a national use rate of 90.7 percent in 2019 (http://bkaprt.com/dfs37/08-08).

Seat belts have come a long way since they were first introduced in the 1950s. The fact that the problem was rooted in automotive companies prioritizing profits over the safety of their users is not lost on me. Designing seat belts for our tech should be the norm and should be enforced through laws and be an expected part in our design work.

The result of legislation mandating seat belts in cars is that the car manufacturers no longer have a choice about whether or not to include them. Imagine the parallel for tech: instead of trying to convince a stakeholder to spend more money on doing the right thing (including a seat belt), that person is already on board, because failing to follow the law comes with real consequences. The idea of a car company trying to skirt the rules and sell a car without seat belts is unfathomable.

We need new policy that establishes requirements around designing for safety, and which enforces consequences to incentivize the adoption of safety practices. Car companies are now held to a wide range of safety standards, including strict protocols around recalls when various parts are later found to have performance issues. Why should it be any different when it comes to tech that enables a stalker to find and murder their victim?

The people who design and build cars, buildings, roads, and parks don't need to worry about convincing their boss to make their product safe because safety is nonnegotiable—there are laws and regulations they have to follow. And while some people do still violate these laws, overall, they work.

This process of normalization—laws requiring seatbelt installation, more laws requiring seatbelt use, and generations of people growing up with seatbelts as routine—took decades. So too will the quest for safe and ethical tech, taken on by people from many different fields. But just as buckling up has become the standard, so too can designing for safety. We have the power to fix the problem of broken tech. We simply need to start.

## Legislating for safer tech

From chemicals in cosmetics to Facebook acting as a news source, allowing industries to self-regulate typically sets the stage for a company to do whatever they want, even when it means people are harmed; just look at car companies and seat belts. If corporations aren't going to act within the best interest of their users, then we need laws that will mandate reasonable efforts to prevent harm and force the tech industry to take the damage it does seriously.

Most of these solutions are not things we can build ourselves, but we can either design them into our products, push other groups within our companies to make changes, or advocate for them outside of our working hours.

- **Model more financial legislation on elder abuse legislation.** Most US states have laws on the books that define the financial abuse of elderly people as a crime that banks are mandated to identify and correct. Because of these laws, banks have practices in place that often include training bankers to recognize the signs of elder abuse and a clear process for escalating suspicions to managers and others who can take action to fix the problem. However, there is no set of practices for the financial abuse of a current or former intimate partner, a situation that prevents many survivors from escaping their abusers. Introducing a law with this focus would be an essential step toward helping survivors regain financial control and leave an abusive partner. The solutions that help prevent financial abuse of the elderly are especially useful here since many of the warning signs are the same in domestic abuse situations.

- **Update stalkerware laws.** Secretly surveilling and tracking others without their consent needs to be illegal. This isn't to say any type of monitoring software should be illegal, as people will argue the right to track devices they own. But covertly monitoring significant others and children isn't a right; it's a violation of their privacy and can have dangerous and even deadly consequences.
- **Make abuse via automobile connectivity illegal.** Currently, there are no laws or regulations addressing the abuse, stalking, and monitoring that happens through modern connected vehicles. In 2016, the NHTSA urged car companies to take safe and appropriate measures against malicious hacking and cyberattacks when designing vehicle systems, but there are no laws in place to enforce these measures. The "cyberattack" framing also ignores the threat model of domestic violence, where abusers typically have access to their victims' devices and knowledge about them that make it a very different threat from an anonymous malicious hacker.
- **Create a safety rating system for IoT devices.** As it stands, there's very little incentive for IoT companies to self-regulate around issues of security and abuse, and users who purchase these products are typically not given information that might help them assess the potential problems with the device. Researchers at University College London have proposed the creation of a ratings system for IoT devices, similar to the energy efficiency ratings that many appliances have (http://bkaprt.com/dfs37/08-09). While such a rating system would not be enough to prevent abuse on its own, it might give potential victims a warning, and would give IoT companies a better incentive to design their products against abuse in the first place.

Part of convincing clients and stakeholders to plan for abuse is presenting a compelling argument that such abuse is not an edge case. We know that harm through these products is already happening, but to fully understand the magnitude and specifics, we need more studies exploring the abuse that happens through financial products, IoT devices, modern automobiles, and products with GPS and location data.

While we as technologists aren't usually the ones doing this research, we can aid in the effort by following the work of researchers working in this space (such as the Gender and IoT project at University College London) and volunteering to partake in interviews or surveys when researchers want to better understand how technologists work and approach these sorts of issues. It's useful to have people in tech speaking out about these issues, raising awareness, and supporting the efforts of groups focused on these types of goals.

## ACTIVISM AND DESIGN

Sometimes a product comes along that's so evil, no amount of thoughtful design can make it safe or inclusive. In these situations, designing for safety means refusing to build the product at all; essentially, to be the gatekeepers of seriously harmful tech.

Victor Papanek was an industrial designer who spearheaded a push for socially just and sustainable design, critiqued consumerism, and wrote the classic text *Design for The Real World*. He was the first to refer to designers as "gatekeepers." Although he wasn't focused specifically on tech (which looked very different in the 1970s when he wrote the book) his call to action remains relevant: that we designers must resist using our skills to create products that are frivolous, useless, or unsafe.

Designer and author Mike Monteiro reinforces this concept when he pushes for designers to act ethically and "be the gatekeepers" in his conference talks and writing. "Working ethically means acting in the best interests of everyone...it means helping those that need the most help," he said in his conference talk, "How to Fight Fascism" (http://bkaprt.com/dfs37/08-10, video).

In that talk, which came in the wake of Donald Trump's early months in office, Monteiro states that certain things can't be designed well because of their enormously negative impact on the most vulnerable:

*You cannot design a good border wall. It is a border wall. It is meant to separate people from each other. You cannot design a good Muslim database. You cannot design a good gun. Because all of these things are inherently evil.*

Put into strict UX terms, some things cannot be designed in a human-centric and empathetic way. And those things should not be built.

I'd like to expand on Papanek's and Monteiro's concept of designers being the gatekeepers: *all* technologists are gatekeepers in some form. A designer may design something that a developer refuses to write the code for; if the developer does write the code for harmful software, a data scientist may refuse to enable proper data processing; and so on. We are all gatekeepers. We can, and should, refuse to design, code, project-manage, and set up data structures for technology that is inherently evil.

## Tech won't build it

Many technologists have been doing just that. In December of 2016, just before Trump met with executives from the country's top tech companies, a group describing themselves as "engineers, designers, business executives, and others whose jobs include managing or processing data about people" signed a pledge to refuse to build a database identifying people based on their race, religion, or national origin (http://bkaprt.com/dfs37/08-11).

Since then, tech activism has continued under the banner of the #TechWontBuildIt hashtag on Twitter. Most notable is the refusal of many tech workers to contribute to the actions carried out by the US Immigration and Customs Enforcement, or ICE:

- Immigrant rights group Mijente created the hashtag #NoTechForIce, which quickly gained traction on Twitter as more and more employees used it to register their resistance toward their employer's connections to the agency.

- More than a thousand Microsoft employees signed a letter asking the company to end their $19.4 million dollar contract with ICE, arguing that the use of the company's tech for facial recognition and data processing allowed the agency to enact "inhumane and cruel policies" (http://bkaprt.com/dfs37/08-12).
- After GitHub renewed its own contract with ICE, not long after its 2018 acquisition by Microsoft, two thousand open source developers signed a letter calling on the company to cancel its contract (http://bkaprt.com/dfs37/08-13).
- In 2019, employees at Tableau, a data visualization company, walked off the job in protest of their company's ties with ICE (http://bkaprt.com/dfs37/08-14).
- That same year, employees at Amazon, Deloitte, and Salesforce organized against their company's relationships with ICE and CBP (US Customs and Border Patrol) (http://bkaprt.com/dfs37/08-15).

A similar situation unfolded at the software company Chef, after the CEO initially resolved to continue working with ICE and CBP despite criticism. He reversed course after a former employee pulled code he had written from Chef's codebase, causing the product to fail for some customers, and current employees continued to push for change (http://bkaprt.com/dfs37/08-16). The fallout of the Chef situation prompted Coraline Ada Ehmke, a speaker, writer, activist, and engineer, to create the Hippocratic License—an "Ethical Source" license that open-source software developers can use to ensure that others cannot use the code they write in software that violates human rights. It has the potential to give open source developers new power in the struggle to keep their code out of the hands of companies who work with ICE (http://bkaprt.com/dfs37/08-17).

There's also been activism in the tech force unrelated to collaboration with ICE. In the early days of 2021, workers at Google and other companies owned by their parent company Alphabet announced the creation of the Alphabet Workers

Union. "We've seen firsthand that Alphabet responds when we act collectively," one project manager at the company said in the release, citing opposition to Project Maven, a project that weaponized AI for use in warfare. Google executives dropped the project after sustained internal resistance (http://bkaprt. com/dfs37/08-18).

All this is to say that far from being apolitical, the long history of engagement and activism among tech workers is alive and well, in some cases after being reignited by the heartless child separation and other policies set by the Trump administration. Technologists are capable of pushing for safe, ethical tech, and although progress isn't always quick or easy, it's important to remember that it is possible.

## Remaining hopeful

The large-scale solutions presented in this chapter are vital—but so are the individual and team-level solutions that make up the previous chapters. A common strategy of naysayers is to downplay the need for whatever immediate change you're advocating for by saying something like, "what we *actually* need is a change in policy." Don't let this tactic of creating a false choice fool you. We don't need to choose between individual-level and system-level changes; we can do both at once.

In fact, we *need* to do both at once. We need to simultaneously work toward big picture solutions while also doing the active day-to-day work of helping users who are being materially harmed right now. If someone tries to interrupt your work designing for safety by saying it's all pointless without bigger changes, remind them that it's possible to do two things at the same time.

Arthur Ashe, the groundbreaking tennis athlete and social activist, said something I find both essential and instructive when starting any kind of important work: "Start where you are. Use what you have. Do what you can."

I think of this quote often. It's common to feel overwhelmed by the enormity of the problem or hopeless in the face of an indifferent team or boss. Fixing our current tech landscape is going to take sustained effort over a long period of time from many people working to slowly transform their teams and companies to prioritize safety, inclusion, and compassion.

If you're the only one on your team who cares about all this, that's okay. Living your values is always a good thing, and you'll find others who will join you if you keep going. You're starting where you are, using what you have, and doing what you can. And even if your individual contribution feels small, it is undoubtedly having an impact.

## WE CAN CHANGE THE WORLD FOR THE BETTER

To truly make designing for safety the norm, we need to make changes both at the individual level and at the systemic level. We must make many small, pointed changes in the everyday way we approach how we design and build technology while also agitating for wider reforms such as laws and regulations, unions, and consequences for company leaders whose products cause harm. This will likely be a decades-long fight, but paradigm shifts of the past show us that with hard work and coordination across fields, it's completely possible to change the world for the better. And the good news is that this work is already well underway. I invite you to join us.

# CONCLUSION

GROWING UP, if I told my grandfather that something was free or cheap—"This shirt was only $10!" or "The trip will be free!"—he'd respond with: "But *how* do you pay?" I didn't understand the question as a child, but as an adult, I think about it constantly. A good deal is never just a good deal; somewhere along the line, someone, or something, pays the true price.

He never laid it out like this, but now I think he was priming me to think about things like oppression, privilege, capitalism, and the interconnectedness of human beings. My ability to get something at a low price cannot be separated from the costs to someone else. My identities and position in society mean that I directly benefit from the exploitation and oppression of other human beings and the planet. Nearly all of us do in some way or another.

In our work as technologists, the cost—of making assumptions about users, of failing to include the people who will be impacted by the product, of just not thinking carefully about our solutions—is that people are harmed. That harm may be minor, or it might be severe. And whether or not our intentions are good, the impact is real.

My hope is that having read this book, you understand how our users are finding ways to subvert the tech we create to harm others, and how to design against that harm. I hope that you are able to bring one or more of the tactics discussed into your daily work; that you're better equipped to talk about these issues with your colleagues and stakeholders; and that you're more ready to say no to building products that no amount of thoughtful design can make ethical. There's a battle being fought for the soul of technology in our society, and you have so much to contribute.

We may not risk our own mental and physical well-being when we decline to put in the work of designing for safety, but we do risk our humanity. Designing for safety will take courage because there are many people out there who would prefer to prioritize profits over safety, and those people work very hard to maintain the status quo. But we owe it to our users we try. We owe it to the unknown but still very real, living, breathing humans who trust us to keep them safe. And I firmly believe that with enough of us pushing this work forward, we can transform the landscape of tech to one that is ethical, inclusive, and safe.

# ACKNOWLEDGMENTS

THANK YOU TO Katel LeDû for taking me on to write a book with my dream publisher, and huge thanks to my editors: Lisa Maria Marquis for brilliantly molding the content of this book into the best shape possible, Sally Kerrigan for her gifted wordsmithing, and Adaobi Obi Tulton for making it all readable. The whole team at ABA is incredible and I am so grateful to all of you.

Erica Garcia, for being my first mentor and setting the groundwork for everything that followed. Shilpa Rao and Jason Early for a quality foundation of UX. Russ Unger, for rejecting my first-ever conference talk proposal and then pulling the abstract for "Designing Against Domestic Violence" out of my brain and telling me to do a talk about that instead. John Allsopp, for helping me understand that this work is valuable. Sara Wachter-Boettcher for helping me figure out how to approach this work, among many other things—if it weren't for you, the proposal for this book would still be sitting on my laptop, unsent.

Mike Monteiro, for being a powerful model for what a designer who is unafraid to live out their ethics within an unethical system looks like. Sasha Costanza-Chock, for writing the incredible book *Design Justice*. Eric Meyer and Sara Wachter-Boettcher (again) for writing *Design for Real Life* and clearly spelling out that we should care about our users. You are the giants on whose shoulders I hope to stand.

Justin, my partner, for being my biggest cheerleader, from attending my very first talk in front of an audience of less than a dozen people to cooking all the healthy meals that fueled writing this book. You're simply the best. Anna Brenner, for all the feedback on my half-formed ideas, snacks, laughter, and confidence-boosting during socially distant porch hangouts. Emily Duma, for endless cross-continental encouragement and for her brilliance on topics of oppression and how they impact tech-facilitated violence and abuse. Maggie Johnson for endless mental health support and vital friendship.

Molly Reynolds, for being an incredible therapist and helping me through many difficulties, and especially for giving me the tools to engage with the terrible realities of domestic violence on a daily basis for years on end without losing hope. The amazing volunteer tech team who helped put together inclusivesafety.com—Leta Keane, Gabriela Voicu, and Sara McMullin for web dev help, Anna Brenner for design, and Amy Holt for curriculum. Kevin Zolk for always investing my git issues. Emma Beuchs, Marleigh Farlow, Cecilie Wian, Chris Cox, Leonie Tanczer, Carmen Pitre, Coraline Ada Ehmke, Per Axbom, and Rob Scott, for sharing their stories and expertise. Jorunn Mjøs for the dozens of helpful links. Resilience, the org that trained me to do rape crisis counseling, for providing outstanding education on sexual assault and domestic violence. Dan Ready for kickstarting my work as a domestic violence educator.

My patrons for financial support through Patreon—you have paid for writing software, access to studies from behind paywalls, membership to domestic violence organizations, and so much more. Thank you from the bottom of my heart.

My incredible design colleagues at 8th Light, for giving me feedback and encouragement on this work over the past five years: Alexa Albanese, Erica Garcia, Daisy Mølving, Julia Murray, Chris Peak, Noah Rogers, Hugh Sato, Kyle Sparks, Gina Valdez, Jon Wettersten, and Kevin Zolkiewicz. Mike Danaher for sharing his expertise on IoT devices, Claudia Richman for vital support (and identifying Tesla safety issues!), and Kristin Kaeding for her tech wisdom. Thank you also to Doug Bradbury, Heather Corrallo, Doug Gapinski, Colin Jones, Kevin Kotowski, Malcolm Newsome, Paul Pagel, and Ryan Verner for the significant workplace support of this work.

Kat, NE, mg, saut, zaly, deer, seau, and everyone else on a certain subreddit who cheered me on through the many rounds of IVF I did while writing this book. Jane Ruffino for understanding. LeagueOfAwesome, TheWebFriends, Hexagon UX, and ConfNerds for community via Slack.

Last but far from least, my family: Caity, for Zoom calls when I needed them most and advice on the nuts and bolts of book writing; Lucas, for casually asking me when I first started this work when I was going to write a book about it; Zach for many laughs; Taryne for always cheering me up; Anna for giving me hope about the next generation of technologists; Mom for being a bottomless well of support; Dad for never letting me lose sight of my mental health; Aunt Patty and Uncle Tom for their astounding generosity; Aunt Jeri for emotional support; and Gma Ruth for constantly telling me not to give up on going after what I want, no matter how high the barriers.

# RESOURCES

I CALL MY WORK "inclusive safety" because I believe safety must be prioritized alongside inclusivity, compassion for our users, and justice; I want safety to include these other aspects rather than sitting in a separate space from them. You can follow along with my work and find links to more resources and learn how to become a volunteer of the Inclusive Safety Project on the project's website (http://bkaprt.com/dfs37/09-01).

## Compassionate, inclusive, and justice-focused design

I think that the ultimate ideal design is not only safe, but also compassionate, inclusive, and just. These books and talks are the perfect starter kit to learn about how to prioritize these values within your design.

- *Design for Real Life* by Eric Meyer and Sara Wachter-Boettcher (http://bkaprt.com/dfs37/05-02)
- *Design for Cognitive Bias* by David Dylan Thomas (http://bkaprt.com/dfs37/09-02)
- *Design Justice* by Sasha Costanza-Chock (http://bkaprt.com/dfs37/07-02)
- "How to Fight Fascism" by Mike Monteiro. This talk, given shortly after the 2016 election of Donald Trump, is a blistering call to arms to designers to be the "gatekeepers" and refuse to build the tech that would allow the new administration to carry out its racist, xenophobic goals, such as a Muslim database (http://bkaprt.com/dfs37/08-10, video).

## Safe remote design research

The Sexual Violence Research Initiative's guide titled *Knowledge Exchange: Pivoting to Remote Research on Violence Against Women During COVID-19* is an invaluable resource for designers doing remote research (http://bkaprt.com/dfs37/06-01, PDF).

## Trauma and trauma-informed design

Trauma-informed design is a new field at the time of writing in 2021, and the leading voice on the matter is the brilliant Theresa Slate. You can follow her work on Twitter (http://bkaprt.com/dfs37/09-03).

When it comes to trauma more generally, the book *The Body Keeps the Score* by Bessel van der Kolk, MD. is a must-read (http://bkaprt.com/dfs37/09-04). The book will help you understand trauma and how it impacts the body and brain. Be warned that it can be an intense read; I suggest reading it in small chunks.

## Race and race in technology

If you're white and work in tech, understanding racism and antiracism is of the utmost importance.

- In the book *How to Be an Antiracist* by Ibram X. Kendi, you'll learn the basics of racism, the larger and more visionary concepts, and how to go beyond simple awareness and begin contributing to a just and equitable society (http://bkaprt.com/dfs37/09-05).
- For a tech-specific lens of racism, read *Race After Technology: Abolitionist Tools for the New Jim Code* by Ruha Benjamin (http://bkaprt.com/dfs37/09-06).

To learn about the societal impact of big data and algorithms and how they reproduce and reinforce existing forms of oppression and inequality, check out the following resources:

- Learn about equitable and accountable artificial intelligence from Joy Adowaa Buolamwini's Algorithmic Justice League (http://bkaprt.com/dfs37/09-07). *Coded Bias*, a documentary about their work, is also well worth your time (http://bkaprt.com/dfs37/09-08).

- *Algorithms of Oppression* by Safiya Umoja Noble lays out the ways that racism, sexism, and other discrimination is embedded in the internet and the algorithms behind search engines such as Google (http://bkaprt.com/dfs37/09-09).
- *Weapons of Math Destruction* by Cathy O'Neil focuses on the social impact of algorithms and how they increasingly reinforce preexisting inequality (http://bkaprt.com/dfs37/09-10).

## Domestic violence

Domestic violence is an enormous, common, and deadly problem in societies around the globe that remains stubbornly out of sight. The following books and articles will help you understand the problem.

- The National Domestic Violence Hotline offers support to survivors via phone call, text, and online chat (http://bkaprt. com/dfs37/09-11). If you saw yourself in any of the stories throughout the book or don't feel safe in your relationship, call or text "START" to 1-800-799-7233 to reach an advocate. Advocates can also assist concerned friends and family as well as abusive partners seeking to change themselves.
- The National Network to End Domestic Violence is a network of state domestic violence organizations and works to address the many aspects of domestic violence. Their website is an incredible resource for learning about the different topics seen in this book, such as financial abuse and stalking, as well as other important information such as safety planning an escape and supporting a loved one in an abusive relationship (http://bkaprt.com/dfs37/09-12).
- *No Visible Bruises: What We Don't Know About Domestic Violence Can Kill Us* by Rachel Louise Snyder is an amazing overview of the problem of domestic violence (http://bkaprt. com/dfs37/09-13).
- *We Do This 'Til We Free Us* by Mariame Kaba is an essential book about abolishing policing and the prison industrial complex and supporting survivors of violence, including domestic violence (http://bkaprt.com/dfs37/09-14). Kaba describes the ways in which the existing system criminalizes

Black women for surviving domestic violence and illustrates that a different future, one that actually supports survivors and transforms abusers, is possible.

- The National Intimate Partner and Sexual Violence Survey from the National Center for Injury Prevention and Control, Centers for Disease Control and Prevention is the big national study where the most recent statistics come from. This is a great document to check out to learn more statistics. It's from 2010, which is getting to be outdated, but it's unfortunately the most recent study of its kind as of 2021 (http://bkaprt.com/dfs37/00-01, PDF).
- "America's Mass Shooting Problem Is a Domestic Violence Problem" summarizes the connection between gun violence and domestic violence: the majority of perpetrators of mass shootings have a history of abusing significant others and family members (http://bkaprt.com/dfs37/09-15).
- Make It Our Business works to ensure that employers meet their domestic violence obligations under OHSA (http://bkaprt.com/dfs37/09-16).

## Domestic violence and harassment online

The following articles and resources will help you understand domestic violence and oppression from technological angles not covered in this book:

- Molly Dragiewicz is a professor of criminology doing vital research on the intersections of domestic violence and technology, with too many important publications to list here. Find her work on tech-facilitated domestic violence and related topics on her website (http://bkaprt.com/dfs37/09-17).
- *Nobody's Victim: Fighting Psychos, Stalkers, Pervs, and Trolls* by Carrie Goldberg covers digital abuse such as partners sending threatening messages, impersonating their former partner, and sharing sexual content without consent (http://bkaprt.com/dfs37/09-18).
- *Sexual Harassment Online: Shaming and Silencing Women in the Digital Age* by Tania G. Levey covers social media harassment

faced by women and how this harassment intersects with race, ethnicity, and class (http://bkaprt.com/dfs37/09-19).

- "Patriarchy Meets Neoliberalism: Tackling Domestic Abuse in the Twenty-First Century" by Elizabeth Yardley is a blog that helps us step back from the details of tech-facilitated domestic violence and place the issue within larger contexts of patriarchy and the ways our society allows and enables certain groups to infringe upon the liberty of other specific groups (http://bkaprt.com/dfs37/01-02).

- Australia's eSafety Office, part of Australia's national government, has the goal of creating safer, more positive experiences online, and focuses especially on women, children, seniors, and diverse groups. It's a great model for what the governments of other countries should be doing to make online spaces safer (http://bkaprt.com/dfs37/09-20).

- *Misogynoir Transformed: Black Women's Digital Resistance* by Moya Bailey explores how Black women, especially queer, nonbinary, gender variant, agender, and trans women, use digital tools to resist misogynoir in various media (http://bkaprt.com/dfs37/09-21).

## Nonconsensual sharing of intimate images

Nonconsensual sharing of intimate images, sometimes known as "revenge porn" or "image abuse," is the sharing of an intimate photo without the subject's consent. It's a growing problem with only a patchwork of state laws, many of which are deeply flawed. The following organizations are working on the issue:

- The Cyber Civil Rights Initiative provides support and technical advice to survivors of image abuse (http://bkaprt.com/dfs37/09-22).
- March Against Revenge Porn is a nonprofit combating nonconsensual image sharing through organizing, legislative action, victim support services, and more. They have a legal defense fund that can help pay the introductory legal fees of survivors of image abuse who would not be able to afford it otherwise (http://bkaprt.com/dfs37/09-23).

## Digital security

Security professionals have a critical role to play in combatting domestic violence and digital abuse:

- Operation Safe Escape is an organization that deploys volunteer security professionals to help vulnerable populations safely escape abusive situations (http://bkaprt.com/dfs37/09-24).
- The Coalition Against Stalkerware works to fight domestic violence, stalking, and harassment through addressing the use of stalkerware (http://bkaprt.com/dfs37/09-25).
- "Hacker Eva Galperin Has a Plan to Eradicate Stalkerware," by Andy Greenberg, explains how antivirus software could play a role in helping victims protect themselves from stalkerware (http://bkaprt.com/dfs37/04-27).
- "'A Stalker's Paradise': How Intimate Partner Abusers Exploit Technology" is a comprehensive study about the specific ways abusers use technology to monitor, stalk, impersonate, harass, threaten, and otherwise harm their victims (http://bkaprt.com/dfs37/09-26, PDF).

# REFERENCES

Shortened URLs are numbered sequentially; the related long URLs are listed below for reference.

## Introduction

**00-01** https://www.cdc.gov/violenceprevention/pdf/nisvs_report2010-a.pdf

**00-02** https://assets.speakcdn.com/assets/2497/dv_in_the_black_community.pdf

**00-03** https://assets.speakcdn.com/assets/2497/american_indian_and_alaskan_native_women__dv.pdf

**00-04** https://www.webmd.com/baby/news/20010320/number-1-cause-of-death-in-pregnant-women-murder

**00-05** https://ncadv.org/blog/posts/quick-guide-to-stalking-16-important-statistics-and-what-you-can-do-about-it

**00-06** https://www.ncoa.org/public-policy-action/elder-justice/elder-abuse-facts/

## Chapter 1

**01-01** https://www.makeuseof.com/tag/alexa-amazon-echo-privacy-risk/

**01-02** https://www.elizabethyardley.com/blog-1/patriarchy-meets-neoliberalism-tackling-domestic-abuse-in-the-twenty-first-century

**01-03** https://www.itpro.co.uk/security/privacy/356759/how-tech-traps-domestic-abuse-victims

**01-04** https://www.apple.com/icloud/find-my/

**01-05** https://www.plannedparenthood.org/learn/relationships/sexual-consent

**01-06** https://www.youtube.com/watch?v=gmGlaEJoIc4

**01-07** https://www.npr.org/sections/alltechconsidered/2014/09/15/346149979/smartphones-are-used-to-stalk-control-domestic-abuse-victims?t=1594764327870

**01-08** https://www.airbnbhell.com/?s=customer+service

## Chapter 2

**02-01** https://www.statista.com/outlook/279/109/smart-home/united-states%23market-revenue

**02-02** https://www.nytimes.com/2018/06/23/technology/smart-home-devices-domestic-abuse.html

02-03    https://www.refinery29.com/en-ca/2019/01/220847/domestic-abuse-vio-
lence-harassment-smart-home-monitoring

02-04    https://www.domesticshelters.org/articles/technology/smart-home-tech-
nology-is-being-used-against-survivors

02-05    https://www.wired.com/2016/08/jeep-hackers-return-high-speed-steer-
ing-acceleration-hacks/

02-06    https://www.huffpost.com/entry/trisha-prabhu-google_n_5675110

02-07    https://www.creativebloq.com/netmag/why-faster-online-experiences-ar-
ent-always-better-81412529

02-08    https://nnedv.org/content/about-financial-abuse/

02-09    https://www.ausbanking.org.au/banks-enhance-support-for-fami-
ly-and-domestic-violence-victims/

02-10    https://twitter.com/internetofshit

02-11    https://www.vice.com/en/article/m7apnn/your-cock-is-mine-now-hacker-
locks-internet-connected-chastity-cage-demands-ransom

02-12    https://www.cnet.com/news/tenants-worry-smart-home-tech-could-be-
abused-by-landlords/

02-13    https://www.nydailynews.com/new-york/brooklyn/ny-facial-rec-
ognition-brownsville-nelson-20190501-5gb32fncjrcmvijwbriimwpc-
sa-story.html

02-14    https://www.wired.com/story/best-algorithms-struggle-recog-
nize-black-faces-equally/

02-15    https://www.forbes.com/sites/parmyolson/2014/04/17/the-quantified-
other-nest-and-fitbit-chase-a-lucrative-side-business/?sh=5f13c1662c8a

## Chapter 3

03-01    https://www.ncbi.nlm.nih.gov/pmc/articles/PMC1447915/

03-02    https://www.vice.com/en/article/gy3kw7/internet-connected-car-technol-
ogy-can-enable-abusers-to-track-victims

03-03    https://www.washingtonpost.com/technology/2019/11/06/womans-stalk-
er-used-an-app-that-allowed-him-stop-start-track-her-car/

03-04    https://twitter.com/MrAndrew/status/1305530276127428609

03-05    https://twitter.com/MrAndrew/status/1307047642510364672

03-06    https://www.wired.com/story/common-apps-domestic-abus-
ers-stalk-victims/

03-07    https://www.abc.net.au/news/2019-11-06/ract-employee-pleads-guilty-to-
using-app-to-stalk-ex-girlfriend/11678980

03-08 https://www.dailymail.co.uk/news/article-7447895/Bumble-stalker-used-FindMyIphone-app-track-victim.html

03-09 https://abc11.com/stalking-ex-wife-ex-husband-iphone-find-me-app/1968446/

03-10 https://support.google.com/maps/search?q=stalking&from_promoted_search=true

03-11 https://blog.superhuman.com/read-statuses/

03-12 https://twitter.com/rahulvohra/status/1146539947655958528

03-13 https://www.theverge.com/2019/7/3/20681508/tracking-pixel-email-spying-superhuman-web-beacon-open-tracking-read-receipts-location

03-14 https://youtu.be/xMXb98N_Up4?t=21660

03-15 https://www.nrk.no/norge/rema-app-kan-misbrukes-til-overvaking-1.15041044

## Chapter 4

04-01 https://www.cbc.ca/news/canada/manitoba/ex-husband-charged-after-winnipeg-woman-finds-hidden-cameras-in-her-home-1.4883215

04-02 https://www.washingtonpost.com/technology/2020/02/18/ring-nest-surveillance-doorbell-camera/

04-03 https://www.buzzfeednews.com/article/salvadorhernandez/home-security-camera-hacked-adt

04-04 https://www.washingtonpost.com/technology/2020/09/24/amazon-ring-security-drone/

04-05 https://www.slashgear.com/ring-always-home-cam-is-a-flying-security-drone-24639740/

04-06 https://www.vice.com/en/article/3a8k79/do-ring-cameras-violate-wiretapping-laws-new-hampshire-is-about-to-find-out

04-07 https://www.npr.org/2019/12/02/784225316/doorbell-cameras-are-popular-but-should-we-be-sharing-the-videos-online

04-08 https://www.vice.com/en/article/d3ag37/us-cities-are-helping-people-buy-amazon-surveillance-cameras-using-taxpayer-money

04-09 https://www.expressnews.com/news/local/article/San-Antonio-domestic-violence-victims-receive-14932616.php

04-10 https://recordinglaw.com/party-two-party-consent-states/illinois-recording-laws/

04-11 https://nymag.com/intelligencer/2020/02/what-its-like-to-own-an-amazon-ring-doorbell-camera.html

04-12   https://www.theguardian.com/technology/2019/dec/27/ring-camera-law-suit-hackers-alabama

04-13   https://gizmodo.com/rings-smart-doorbell-let-a-man-spy-on-his-ex-boy-friend-1825963112

04-14   https://stopstalkerware.org/what-is-stalkerware/

04-15   https://www.nytimes.com/2018/05/19/technology/phone-apps-stalking.html

04-16   https://www.sun-sentinel.com/news/crime/fl-miramar-cid-torrez-more-charges-20140808-story.html

04-17   https://www.welivesecurity.com/2014/04/03/domestic-spyware-apps-increasingly-precursor-to-violence-or-murder/

04-18   https://www.independent.co.uk/life-style/gadgets-and-tech/fbi-shuts-down-stealthgenie-invisible-stalker-app-9769849.html

04-19   https://www.bryanfagan.com/family-law-blog/2016/january/cell-phones-mail-computers-spying-on-your-spouse/

04-20   https://www.congress.gov/bill/109th-congress/house-bill/744/text

04-21   https://www.nytimes.com/2016/11/10/style/family-digital-surveil-lance-tracking-smartphones.html

04-22   https://nautil.us/issue/35/boundaries/parents-shouldnt-spy-on-their-kids

04-23   https://www.tiktok.com/@christneko/video/6704066255717928198?lang-Country=en

04-24   https://www.theguardian.com/sustainable-business/2015/nov/05/par-ents-children-online-search-history-microsoft-windows-10-privacy

04-25   https://letgrow.org/teen-phone-monitoring/

04-26   https://digitalcommons.law.seattleu.edu/sjsj/vol15/iss1/15/

04-27   https://www.wired.com/story/eva-galperin-stalkerware-kasper-sky-antivirus/

## Chapter 5

05-01   http://scholar.google.com/

05-02   https://abookapart.com/products/design-for-real-life

05-03   https://www.huffpost.com/entry/google-black-people-goril_n_7717008

05-04   https://journals.aom.org/doi/abs/10.5465/amj.2014.0538

05-05   https://www.cnbc.com/2020/06/12/six-years-into-diversity-reports-big-tech-has-made-little-progress.html

# Chapter 6

06-01 https://www.svri.org/sites/default/files/attachments/2020-07-23/SVRI Knowledge Exchange - Research VAW COVID - Final.pdf

# Chapter 7

07-01 https://news.yahoo.com/dr-phil-backed-domestic-violence-184656426.html

07-02 https://mitpress.mit.edu/books/design-justice

07-03 https://www.ucl.ac.uk/steapp/research/digital-technologies-policy-laboratory/gender-and-iot

# Chapter 8

08-01 https://www.reddit.com/r/AmItheAsshole/comments/hzr160/aita_for_being_angry_at_my_husband_for_spending/

08-02 https://www.reddit.com/r/AmItheAsshole/comments/jbswil/new_resources_for_anyone_looking_to_help_those_in/

08-03 https://www.nbcnews.com/tech/social-media/timeline-facebook-s-privacy-issues-its-responses-n859651

08-04 https://www.nytimes.com/2019/07/09/opinion/email-tracking.html

08-05 https://www.history.com/this-day-in-history/unsafe-at-any-speed-hits-bookstores

08-06 https://www.nytimes.com/2015/11/27/automobiles/50-years-ago-unsafe-at-any-speed-shook-the-auto-world.html

08-07 https://crashstats.nhtsa.dot.gov/Api/Public/ViewPublication/810962

08-08 https://www.nhtsa.gov/risky-driving/seat-belts

08-09 https://www.ucl.ac.uk/jill-dando-institute/research-projects/2020/aug/developing-consumer-security-index-domestic-iot-devices-csi

08-10 https://www.youtube.com/watch?v=vW2moFk074Q

08-11 https://neveragain.tech/

08-12 https://www.usnews.com/news/politics/articles/2018-06-20/microsoft-employees-demand-company-end-contract-with-ice

08-13 https://www.theatlantic.com/technology/archive/2020/01/ice-contract-github-sparks-developer-protests/604339/

08-14 https://www.geekwire.com/2019/tableau-employees-hold-rally-seattle-ask-leadership-sever-ties-ice-cbp/

08-15    https://www.forbes.com/sites/rachelsandler/2019/07/19/amazon-sales-
force-wayfair-employees-stage-internal-protests-for-working-with-
ice/?sh=474018453e94

08-16    https://www.wired.com/story/software-company-chef-wont-renew-
ice-contact/

08-17    https://firstdonoharm.dev/

08-18    https://alphabetworkersunion.org/press/releases/2021-01-04-code-cwa-
google-union/

## Resources

09-01    https://www.inclusivesafety.com/

09-02    https://abookapart.com/products/design-for-cognitive-bias

09-03    https://twitter.com/theresaslateis

09-04    https://www.besselvanderkolk.com/resources/the-body-keeps-the-score

09-05    https://www.ibramxkendi.com/how-to-be-an-antiracist/

09-06    https://www.wiley.com/en-us/Race+After+Technology:+Abolition-
ist+Tools+for+the+New+Jim+Code-p-9781509526437

09-07    http://ajl.org/

09-08    https://www.ajl.org/spotlight-documentary-coded-bias

09-09    http://algorithmsofoppression.com/

09-10    https://weaponsofmathdestructionbook.com/

09-11    https://www.thehotline.org/

09-12    https://nnedv.org/

09-13    https://www.bloomsbury.com/us/no-visible-bruises-9781635570977/

09-14    https://www.indiebound.org/book/9781642595253

09-15    https://www.huffpost.com/entry/mass-shooters-domestic-vio-
lence_n_5a0376e7e4b0937b510f5fdd

09-16    http://makeitourbusiness.ca/

09-17    https://www.mollydragiewicz.com/dv-tech-study-info

09-18    https://www.nobodys-victim.com/

09-19    http://tanialevey.com/new-book/

09-20    https://www.esafety.gov.au/

09-21    https://nyupress.org/9781479890491/misogynoir-transformed/

09-22    https://www.cybercivilrights.org/

09-23    https://marchagainstrevengeporn.org/our-vision

09-24    https://safeescape.org/

09-25    https://stopstalkerware.org/

09-26    http://nixdell.com/papers/stalkers-paradise-intimate.pdf

# INDEX

## A

abuser testing 79
account ownership 20-26, 22-23
activism and design 119-122
AI facial recognition 28
Airbnb 11, 89
Albergotti, Reed 59
Amazon Echo Drop In 4-5
Apple Find My 9, 39, 40
archetypes 73-75
Ashe, Arthur 122
Aspire News app 99-101
assumptions 108-109

## B

Black Mirror brainstorm 76
Bloomstein, Margot 18
Boyd, Danah 64-65
brainstorming problems 76

## C

cameras and recording 56
centering impacted communities
    102-105
Coalition Against Stalkerware 61
community control 105
consent 8-9, 46-48
Costanza-Chock, Sasha 103, 105-106
Cox, Chris 6
Crayton, Kim 69
creating change 112-115
Crenshaw, Kimberlé Williams 104
customer support 25-26

## D

designing for safety 1, 106-109
design justice 81
design solutions 77-78
digital vs. physical control 27-29
diversity, equity, and inclusion (DEI)
    86
domestic violence viii
Dr. Phil 99

## E

Ehmke, Coraline Ada 121
Electronic Frontier Foundation 68
empathy in research 89-90

## F

Facebook 111, 117
Farlow, Marleigh 49
financial abuse 19
flagging abusive activity 19-20

## G

Galperin, Eva 68
gaslighting 30
getting uncomfortable 83
Google Photos 84
Google Scholar 72
Greenberg, Andy 39

## H

Hippocratic License 121
history logs 30-31

## I

identify verification 49-50
impact and intent 12
internet of things (IoT) 29
Internet Spyware Prevention Act 64
interpersonal harm x
interviewing vulnerable users 90-95
intimate partner violence viii

## L

Land Rover 39
laws and law enforcement issues
    57-58
legal gray areas 63-64
legal information for users 58
legislating for safer tech 117-118
location-sharing 39-43

## M

McGraw, Robin 99
Meyer, Eric 80
Mjøs, Jorunn 24
Monteiro, Mike 119

## N

Nader, Ralph 115
National Coalition for the Homeless 67
National Gay and Lesbian Task Force Policy Institute 67
National Highway Traffic Safety Administration (NHTSA) 115
Nest thermostat 11, 14-15
Nguyen, Christina 67

## O

Olsen, Erica 35
Open Web Application Security Project's (OWASP) 60
organizational support 81-84

## P

Papanek, Victor 119
password problems 59-60
passwords 7
physical fallbacks 29
Pitre, Carmen 7
privacy settings 38
Process for Inclusive Safety 70-80, 81

## R

regulation 115-118
remote harassment 16-20
remote interviewing 94-95
research approaches 71-72
Ring 10, 55-56, 57, 59, 63

## S

security best practices 60
Seward, Andrew 35-36
Sexual Violence Research Initiative 94
Siminoff, Jamie 60
Slate, Theresa 101
Southworth, Cindy 16
spyware and children 64-67
stalkerware 61-68
stalking 34-38, 43-46, 47, 51
standardizing safe design 113-114
Strava Flyby 36-37
stress testing 80
Superhuman 43-45
supporting diverse teams 84-86
surveillance 10-11, 47, 53
    Amazon-enabled 55-56
survivor testing 79-80

## T

Tanczer, Leonie 107
tech abuse ix
technologist x
technology-facilitated coercive control ix
technology-facilitated domestic violence (TFDV) ix
TechWontBuildIt 120
Tesla 11, 23, 27-28
testing for safety 78-80
tracking pixels 45-46
trauma-informed design 101-102

## U

user experience and user safety 48-50
using location data 46
using statistics 83

## V

van der Kolk, Bessel 106
vicarious trauma (coping with)
    96–97
victim vs. survivor ix
Vohra, Rahul 43

## W

Wachter-Boettcher, Sara 80
Warzel, Charlie 112
Wian, Cecilie 46–47

## Y

Yardley, Elizabeth 5

## Z

Zuckerberg, Mark 111

## ABOUT A BOOK APART

We cover the emerging and essential topics in web design and development with style, clarity, and above all, brevity—because working designer-developers can't afford to waste time.

## COLOPHON

The text is set in FF Yoga and its companion, FF Yoga Sans, both by Xavier Dupré. Headlines and cover are set in Titling Gothic by David Berlow.

 This book was printed in the United States using FSC certified papers.